Duke University Press ■ Durham and London 2002

Anecdotal Theory   Jane Gallop

© 2002 Duke University Press ■ All rights reserved

Printed in the United States of America on acid-free paper ∞

Designed by Rebecca Giménez ■ Typeset in Adobe Minion by

Keystone Typesetting, Inc. ■ Library of Congress Cataloging-in-

Publication Data appear on the last printed page of this book.

For Chris Amirault who—

over the decade of this writing—

taught me the relation

between anecdote and theory

Contents

Acknowledgments

I would like here to express my gratitude to three men whose belief in *Anecdotal Theory* helped me believe in it:

Ken Wissoker, my editor, who first thought it could in fact be a book;

Joe Litvak—*mon semblable, mon frère,* my ideal reader—who gave me in advance the dream response that made it all worthwhile; and

Jeff King, my companion throughout the work on this book, whose invaluable assistance always combined enthusiasm for my ideas with stalwart refusal of my lazy formulations.

And I am inclined to say that our theorizing (and I intentionally use the verb rather than the noun) is often in narrative forms, in the stories we create, in riddles and proverbs, in the play with language, since dynamic rather than fixed ideas seem more to our liking.

Dynamic ideas are definitely more to my liking. Through the decade of the nineties, my own theorizing sought a form of writing that could honor this preference. In order to inscribe my perhaps idiosyncratic attempts within a larger effort—something someone might call "*our* theorizing"—I begin with this sentence from Barbara Christian's mid-eighties essay "The Race for Theory."[1]

Written in the heyday of "theory" in the U.S. literary academy (that moment in the mid-eighties when deconstructive, poststructuralist discourse seemed predominant), Christian's essay spoke forcefully to and of its moment, quickly becoming notorious (and oft reprinted) as an attack on "theory." What is less frequently noted is that Christian rejects not theory per se but a certain kind of theory—that the essay also advocates an alternative way of theorizing.

Christian champions the claims of literature against a theory which is to her mind grotesquely unliterary: "And as a student of literature, I am appalled by the sheer ugliness of the language . . . its lack of pleasurableness" (230). The irony is that literary scholars should foster such unliterary theory.

In contrast to the theory which appalls Christian, "our theorizing is often in narrative forms, stories, riddles, proverbs, the play with language." The kind of theorizing Christian prefers is what we might want to call Literary Theory—if by that phrase we understood not a theory of literature, but a theory that was itself truly literary. The essays I collect in this volume are my attempt—after and in response to that eighties "theory" moment—to produce a more literary theory.

■   ■   ■

During the nineties I experimented with writing in which I would recount an anecdote and then attempt to "read" that account for the theoretical insights it afforded. It is this particular practice of theorizing that I want to indicate by the title *Anecdotal Theory*. Although not all of the essays included in this volume follow this pattern, they all belong to a period when I was trying to think through anecdote. In this introduction, I would like to situate this project of anecdotal theory, to indicate some of its presumptions and implications.

An anecdote, my dictionary informs me, is "a short account of some interesting or humorous incident." While the writing in this volume often has the "humorous" tone typical of anecdote, the anecdotes become "interesting" precisely for their ability to intervene in contemporary theoretical debates. "Anecdote" and "theory" carry diametrically opposed connotations: humorous vs. serious, short vs. grand, trivial vs. overarching, specific vs. general. Anecdotal theory would cut through these oppositions in order to produce theory with a better sense of humor, theorizing which honors the uncanny detail of lived experience.

In "The History of the Anecdote," Joel Fineman defines the anecdote as "the narration of a singular event" and insists on its literary nature. If Fineman's "History" must insist on the literary nature of the anecdote, it is because of its unique place in the literary: it is, according to him, "the literary form or genre that uniquely refers to the real. . . . The anecdote, however literary, is nevertheless directly pointed towards or rooted in the real."[2]

Fineman, Christian's colleague at Berkeley, delivered "The History of the Anecdote" just a year after "The Race for Theory" was first presented at a conference.[3] Fineman could well represent the "theory" Christian was writing against. His essay is an excellent example of mid-eighties deconstructionist theorizing. However perverse it might seem, I read the two essays together because they belong to the same moment of the U.S. literary academy, the moment that lays the groundwork for the theoretical writing in the present volume. If I emphasize the two essays' proximity in place and time, it is because I find their proximity deliciously anecdotal (as I try to imagine Christian and Fineman crossing paths and conversing in Berkeley in the eighties).[4]

Fineman prizes the anecdote because it is at one and the same time literary and real. And although Christian would seem to be opposed to the very sort of theory that Fineman's essay represents, she too prizes both the literary and the real. Fineman's approach is psychoanalytic and deconstructive, high poststructuralist theory (his texts are all by European men); Christian speaks in the name of feminism and people of color. Although apparently opposed in this mid-eighties moment, both would like to interrupt what is too fixed, too abstract, too eternal and ahistorical by looking to the place where the literary is knotted to the real.

If in this introduction I emphasize the moment, it is because the anecdotal is very much about the moment. By laying stress on the theoretical moment, I'm trying to move toward an anecdotal relation to theory. Locating Christian and Fineman despite their opposition (or maybe because of it) within the same theoretical moment repeats the gesture of one of the essays in this book.

"Dating Derrida in the Nineties" locates Derrida's 1972 reading of women in Nietzsche as belonging to the same moment as what it opposes (a seventies feminist celebration of a too singular "woman"). This essay appears in the part of this collection entitled "The Stories" because emphasis on the moment is a crucial piece of telling stories about theory. Emphasis on the moment is crucial for anecdotalizing theory.

"Dating Derrida" was written in 1992 and reads the marks of 1972 in Derrida's text in order to think the relation between those two dates. The twenty-year span figures what we call a generation, and the essay muses generational relations—not in the predominant familial model but according to a pedagogical model. In 1972 I began graduate school and read Derrida for the first time; in 1992 I produced this reading of Derrida while teaching him to graduate students. My theorizing in this essay is framed by an intergenerational encounter in the classroom (the story of my relation to my student Ellen)[5] in such a manner that we see how the pedagogical encounter gave rise to the theorizing. Appearing in most if not all the essays in this volume, the pedagogical relation is perhaps the central drama of my theorizing in the nineties.

"Dating Derrida" thinks in particular about and through the relation between deconstruction and feminism. Reading the traces in Derrida's text of the relation between seventies feminism and deconstruction (a relation which has become a familiar part of the history of theory), the essay is trying to figure out the relation between deconstruction and feminism in the nineties. My project of anecdotal theory would have to be located at the intersection of deconstruction and feminism.

The final piece in the collection—"Econstructing Sisterhood," written in 1999—has in its very title the eroded trace of the encounter between feminism and (d)econstruction (deconstruction is eroded because a bit passé). That essay is both a contribution to feminist theory (an attempt to think through the question of sisterhood and the problem of difference between women) and an "occasional piece," written for the occasion of my sister's fiftieth birthday. The coincidence of my sister's birthday with the date of a conference on Feminism and Rhetoric in the city where she lives occasioned my theorizing, just as the classroom encounter with Ellen occasioned the theorizing in 1992. In both essays, I first wanted simply to dedicate the writing to the woman who inspired my thinking, but

I went on and tried to make the dedication integral, intrinsic to the theorizing.

While it is the feminist in me who claims recognition for the women who make me think, deconstruction seconds the gesture by insisting on the "occasional," on the event, the moment, as the site of productive thinking. As I put it in "Econstructing," "dedications and occasional pieces are rhetorical sites where discourse is knotted to the extradiscursive, to the here and now, to real life." Like anecdotes, according to Fineman, occasional pieces are a literary form or genre rooted in and pointing toward the real.

Although writing in honor of a birthday is more typical of the literary genre, in fact all the essays in this volume are occasional pieces. All were written for particular academic events; all were conceptualized in response to invitations to speak at conferences or publish on specific topics. The present book is a collection of occasional theory, theorizing produced at a particular moment for a particular context. Rather than consider such occasional theory as a failure to achieve the ideal of abstract, universally applicable, timeless theory, I would argue that it provides the opportunity to knot theory to the here and now.

My 1999 celebration of the "occasional" at a feminist conference occasioned my belated "coming-out" as a deconstructionist: "Call me a deconstructionist if you like, but personally I don't take rhetorical gestures as frosting spread on top of thought; I take rhetoric to be the very place where thought happens." The rhetorical gesture "Call me a deconstructionist if you like, but personally . . . " is repeated in the talk, providing a sort of comic refrain—comic in taking deconstruction "personally." Although deconstruction was often held to be in opposition to the sort of personal discourse favored by seventies feminism, by the nineties it became possible to recognize a deconstructionist personal and speak a personalized deconstruction. My project of anecdotalizing theory is located very much at this intersection of the deconstructionist with the personal.

"The personal" is in fact the topic of the very first sentence of the first essay in *Anecdotal Theory*: "If the adjective 'personal,' elevated to noun status, has become a central focus for pedagogical theory, it is singularly due to something called 'feminist teaching.' " The essay that begins with this sentence was written for a conference on Pedagogy and the Question of the Personal. Drafted in 1992 just a month before I wrote "Dating Derrida," that essay is likewise about how theorizing arises in the pedagogical encounter.

The opening essay of the volume not only introduces the pedagogical relation which will play such a central role in the collection but also provides a model for anecdotal theory, an explicitly feminist model. The first anecdote in the book is a story from the classroom, not from my classroom but from Helene Keyssar's feminist theater production course at the University of California, San Diego in 1982.

In an essay entitled "Staging the Feminist Classroom: A Theoretical Model," Keyssar recounts a classroom incident and explicitly grounds her theorizing in that incident, analyzing the moment for its theoretical implications. Finding the incident particularly rich with implications, I return to Keyssar's anecdote to continue the theorizing she begins. Her essay is a good example of mid-eighties feminist writing about teaching. Opening this collection with my reading of Keyssar stages her essay as a sort of theoretical prototype, marking how the practice of anecdotal theory derives from feminist teaching.

I entitle the first section of this collection "The Incident" because, like Keyssar, I ground my theoretical writing in incidents, especially pedagogical incidents. "The Incident" opens with my reading of Keyssar and closes with another essay based in a story about a student and a teacher. In the latter case, I learned about the story not by reading but because I know the teacher personally. She told me her story and (with her permission) I recount it in order to unpack its theoretical implications.

That essay ("Resisting Reasonableness") talks about why I tell this story of a student-teacher couple. What I say there articulates some of the goals of anecdotal theory: "Rather than reach a general understanding via the norm, I choose to theorize via a relatively rare and marginal case. I'm trying to theorize pedagogy in a way that resists the norm, a way of theorizing that I want to call exorbitant. This paper takes as its pedagogical model the couple I began with. It is, to be sure, an exorbitant model."

Anecdotal theory is what in this 1998 essay I called exorbitant theorizing (like Christian, "intentionally using the verb rather than the noun"). The usual presupposition of theory is that we need to reach a general understanding, which then predisposes us toward the norm, toward a case or model that is prevalent, mainstream. To dismiss something as "merely anecdotal" is to dismiss it as a relatively rare and marginal case. Anecdotal theory would base its theorizing on exorbitant models.

"Resisting Reasonableness" explicitly associates "exorbitant" with the excessive, romantic, perverse, unreasonable, and queer. But the word carries with it a very specific allusion which remains unspoken in the essay. In the middle of Derrida's *Of Grammatology,* the book in which he sets out his program for deconstruction, is a methodological statement entitled "The Exorbitant. Question of Method." The model for exorbitant theorizing is Derrida.

Derrida has chosen as his example a little known text by Rousseau, a "relatively rare and marginal" text. In the context of justifying the weight given to this example, he imagines critics dismissing his method as "exorbitant": "We are preparing to privilege, in a manner that some will not fail to judge exorbitant, certain texts."[6] Rather than defend himself against these imagined charges, he goes on to assert, "Our choice is in fact *exorbitant*" (emphasis Derrida's). Brazenly embracing a term he first imagines being used against him, Derrida employs a rhetorical gesture often used by militant marginal groups, as in the recent adoption of the term *queer,* among others.

Refusing to be shamed, not only does Derrida claim the term but he shouts it, places it in italics. He then goes on to write a one-sentence paragraph all in italics: "*But what is the exorbitant?*" This exceedingly short italicized paragraph stylistically enacts exorbitance.

In his next paragraph, Derrida answers that question etymologically: from the Latin, "ex-," out of, and "orbita," route or orbit.

The paragraph plays with routes, orbits, and orbs ("our theorizing is in the play with language"). Picking up on the meaning of the prefix "ex-," Derrida associates "the exorbitant" with exteriority, with exits, departures, attempts to get out, and in particular with the attempt to get out of a rut.[7] The rut he wants to get out of is the rut philosophy is in, the metaphysical rut which separates philosophy (or what we would call theory) from empiricism (the link to the real, the here and now). Derrida connects the exorbitant with the attempt to get outside the metaphysical closure that sequesters theory from the real.

The anecdotal is exorbitant. While never using Derrida's adjective, Fineman describes the anecdote in terms of the same constellation of excess, opening, and access to the real: "There is something about the anecdote that exceeds its literary status, and this excess is precisely that which gives the anecdote its pointed, referential access to the real."

The anecdote, according to Fineman, not only is excessive but by that excess "introduces an opening." Fineman goes on to describe this opening in very sexy terms: as "the seductive opening of anecdotal form," and as "the opening that is effected by the anecdote, the hole and rim—using psychoanalytic language, the orifice—traced out by the anecdote."

Fineman in fact suggests that there is something intrinsically erotic about the anecdote. He refers to "an anecdotal history that lives up to the erotics of its name." Since the name of this history is *Anekdota,* he implies that the word "anecdote" promises an erotics. Telling us that *Anekdota* is "usually referred to as *Secret History*" and mentioning that "anecdote" means etymologically "that which is 'unpublished'" further suggests that the erotics of the anecdotal is tied to what is secret or unpublished.[8]

In the present volume the anecdotal does turn out to be rather insistently sexual. Starting with the very first essay, "The Teacher's Breasts," the anecdotes that give rise to theorizing tend more often than not to be incidents in which sex emerges in an intellectual, professional, or pedagogical scene. Anecdotal theory is theory grappling with its erotics.

While this collection certainly bears out Fineman's deconstructionist sense of anecdotal opening as erotic, it also contains an explicitly feminist sense of anecdotal opening. And the latter is pretty much in direct opposition to the emergence of the erotic in the intellectual sphere. The third essay of this collection, addressing the question of sex in the academy, has occasion to quote from Catharine MacKinnon's landmark treatise on sexual harassment, the 1979 book that more than any other defined the issue. The MacKinnon passage I quote in that essay turns out to contain its own version of anecdotal opening:

> I hope to bring to the law something of the reality of women's lives. The method and evidence chosen for this task deserve comment. . . . Women's consciousness erupts through fissures in the socially knowable. Personal statements direct from daily life, in which we say more than we know, may be the primary form in which such experiences exist in social space: at this point they may be their only accessible form.[9]

"Erupts through fissures" is a striking image of opening; "personal statements direct from daily life" are anecdotal.

Like Derrida, MacKinnon feels the need to comment on her "method and evidence," knowing that traditionalists will dismiss the evidence as anecdotal and the method as exorbitant. MacKinnon values anecdotal evidence because, like Fineman, she is interested in access to the real. MacKinnon's methodological statement is recognizably feminist: "women's consciousness," "the reality of women's lives." I read her statement as arguing for the validity of anecdotal theory in feminist terms—which is why I include it here in this introduction.

I also include it because I take perverse pleasure in its resemblance to Fineman and Derrida. I believe the resemblance to be not just coincidental but theoretical. I believe it reflects a broader shared project, the project of making knowledge that better opens to the real—a project that can include aspects of both feminism and deconstruction. My rhetorical coupling of MacKinnon and Derrida repeats my earlier coupling of Fineman with Christian. Between the two gestures, I have tried to locate anecdotal theory at the cross-roads of deconstruction and feminism, tried to insist on its dual heritage.

I am, I must confess, just too drawn to the figure of the couple, especially this sort of couple, a male-female odd couple. As much as I want to recognize this as the mark of my sexuality in my theory, I also want to remain wary of its blindnesses. In this case, it has made me reduce the intellectual derivation of anecdotal theory to two (gender-binarized) terms.

To the neatly gendered couple of feminism and deconstruction, we have to add a third term, psychoanalysis. In setting up this introduction, I've tended to assimilate psychoanalysis to deconstruction—I characterized Fineman as both deconstructionist and psychoanalytic—but in fact deconstruction and psychoanalysis are not so easily interchangeable. The relation between the two is in fact a question in this volume, not an assumption.

The very earliest essay in this collection—the opening piece of the second section—worries the relation between deconstruction and psychoanalysis. Entitled "A Tale of Two Jacques," that 1991 essay features an odd couple, but this one is not male-female; the essay is about Derrida and Lacan. "A Tale" was my earliest attempt at anecdotal theory. But the tale it recounts—the first of "The Stories"—is of a very odd sort of incident, not an event that occurred in real life but not exactly a fiction either. "A Tale of Two Jacques" recounts a dream I had.

As I say in that essay, the fantasy behind its method is "an interpretation of dreams where dreams interpret theory rather than vice versa." But then I realize that method is not just a fantasy; it is psychoanalytic method. Freud used his dreams to theorize; he did not just take his dreams as evidence of his theory but theorized in his sleep. For example, he credits a dream he had with the discovery of the Oedipus complex. Freud showed us how dreams theorize in riddles and in the play with language, two examples Christian gives of the sort of literary theorizing that is "more to our liking." Freud theorized the psyche based on dreams, slips, jokes; likewise, he theorized sexuality based on perversions rather than the reproductive norm. His insistence on theorizing based in marginal rather than "normal" activity is a model of exorbitant theorizing. At its least normative, at its best, psychoanalysis is an anecdotal theory: by grounding theory in case history, psychoanalysis demands that theory test itself against the uncanny details of story.

"A Tale of Two Jacques" is an occasional piece; like all the essays in this book, it arose in response to a particular theoretical occasion. In March of 1991 I got a phone call inviting me to present a paper for a conference session on Lacan and Derrida Revisited. That night I had a dream. Six months later, rereading Derrida's 1974 article on Lacan in order to write the paper, I recalled the dream and began to feel it was a sort of reading of Derrida's text. Bringing my dream into the paper, using it as a reading of Derrida and Lacan, was my attempt to theorize from a different place.

The place I mean is not actually the land of dreams. Although my first attempt at anecdotal theory thinks through a dream, none of the other essays do. I want to theorize from a place where dreams cohabit with a host of other narrative forms, riddles, and stories, and play with language. Not dreams as otherworldly but dreams as one opening, among others, where we connect to the here and now.

"A Tale of Two Jacques" recounts the mid-seventies encounter between deconstruction and psychoanalysis as a drama I lived through. Like "Dating Derrida" (written a year later), the earliest essay in this collection understands theory in relation to its moments. That awareness of the moment makes it possible to tell the story of theorizing. All of these essays tell stories of how theory is lived by the theorizing subject, how theory takes place as the passions and dramas of that life.

Anecdotal theory is not only theorizing on the basis of anecdote —which, however exorbitant the anecdotal example, still leaves unchallenged the traditional relation between theory and example. Beyond theorizing anecdote, I would hope to find the seductive fissures in theory. Beyond theorizing anecdote, I would hope to anecdotalize theory—to make theorizing more aware of its moment, more responsible to its erotics, and at the same time, if paradoxically, both more literary and more real.

Part One The Incident

■ ■ ■

The essays in this volume come from three distinct periods: there are four essays from 1991–92, two pieces written in 1994, and three written in 1998–99. The chronology of these essays—and especially the gaps between the three periods—indicate a story.

Part 2 of the collection, "The Stories," includes three of the earliest essays and the two most recent ones, and none from the middle of the decade. The pieces in part 2 are the clearest examples of anecdotal theory: all attempt explicitly to ground their theory in stories from my life.

The first three essays in part 2 were written between November 1991 and September 1992. Although they differ considerably in theoretical topic as well as in the type of personal incident recounted, all three include memoir in their theorizing. Taken together, the three pieces explore the possibility of writing theory explicitly from the subjectivity of the theorizing subject, theorizing from the lived moment. By fall of 1992, I was thus launched on the project of anecdotal theory.

In November 1992, that project was interrupted. I learned I had been accused of sexual harassment by two of my graduate students. The university investigation did not reach its final resolution until

February 1994. After that experience, I felt compelled to theorize about what I had been forced to learn. I spent the next four years writing about sexual harassment policy in the academy and its implications for the pursuit of knowledge. It was not until late in 1998 that I was able to get back to the project of anecdotal theorizing I had been pursuing in 1992.

Looking now at this interruption to anecdotal theory, I find it ironic. I was embarked on a theoretical project which aimed to tie theorizing to lived experience. And then that theoretical project was interrupted, derailed, by lived experience. Although I can't say that I like it, I can see that it is precisely this ability to interrupt and divert a project conceived in theory which makes incident a force with which theory must reckon. I can see that anecdotal theory must be, whether or not I like it, this juncture where theory finds itself compelled—against its will, against its projects—to think where it has been forced to think.

Theory has a considerable will to power; it wants to comprehend all it surveys. Theory tends to defend against what threatens that sense of mastery. Theory likes to set up an ideal realm where it need encounter no obstacle to the expansion of its understanding. By bracketing the incidents and situations in which it finds itself, theory can feel the exhilarating power to think untrammeled by feeling, life, and context. But this power is abstract, Pyrrhic. As heady as I find the freedom of that abstract power, I seek a more effective power. I theorize not just to feel powerful but in order better to negotiate the world in which I find myself.

Anecdotal theory drags theory into a scene where it must struggle for mastery. Theorizing in explicit relation to the here and now, theorizing because the subject feels the need to, theory must contend with what threatens its mastery. Subjecting theory to incident teaches us to think in precisely those situations which tend to disable thought, forces us to keep thinking even when the dominance of our thought is far from assured.

Part 1, "The Incident," consists of theory I wrote in response to my being accused of sexual harassment. This theorizing is thus also anecdotal, but in a different way. An anecdote can be defined as "a short account of an incident." Whereas the second part of this collection grounds its theorizing in such accounts, the first part contains theory grounded in an incident, although that incident is not narrated in writing the theory.

The writing in part 1 is more typical of how anecdotal theory usually exists in the world: while the impetus for theorizing is often the need to think through a life occurrence, the occurrence is generally not included as part of the theorizing (although it may sometimes be alluded to in prefatory material). If one includes the essays in the first part of the book in the concept of anecdotal theory, then a whole lot of theory turns out to be "anecdotal": that is, the thinking is inspired, energized, or made necessary by some puzzling, troubling, instigating life event.

The second essay in part 1, "*The Lecherous Professor*," was written in 1994, immediately after my experience of being investigated for sexual harassment. It is a close, symptomatic reading of a feminist text, the sort of critical reading I'd been doing for two decades, the kind of work upon which I had built my scholarly reputation. Written for an academic conference, the essay was an attempt to bring the topic of sexual harassment into the domain of my expertise. Turning my methodology on a text which represented the discourse under which I had been accused was an attempt in theory to reassert the mastery the investigation had taken from me.

Rereading the essay now, I don't much like it; I find it bitter and adversarial. I prefer reading to explore a text, but this essay is not exploration, it is investigation. Like the investigation I had just undergone, the essay goes about trying to determine good and evil, looking for evidence of harm and finding culpability. I can see now what I could not see then: that it represents a fantasy reversal, the fantasy that I could turn the tables on my judges (the feminists making and enforcing harassment policy). That fantasy dictates the terms of the reading: I had been accused not only of sexual harassment but of discrimination on the basis of sexual orientation (the students filing complaints were both lesbians); my reading of *The Lecherous Professor* accuses harassment policymakers of homophobia and heterosexism.

Rereading the essay for this collection, I have been tempted to leave it out. I have decided to keep it in because it represents an important, if not very appealing, aspect of anecdotal theory. This is not the anecdotal theory I am proud of; it is the anecdotal theory that embarrasses me. I see myself in this essay struggling to theorize there where I feel so embattled. The writing and the thought are marred by the strident tone of my desperation. This may be anecdotal theory more as acting out than as working through.

If in the present context of proclaiming anecdotal theory this essay embarrasses me, it seems worth noting that the essay displays its own embarrassment at the anecdotal nature of its theory. In the 1994 introduction to the piece, I wrote: "In the last two years I have had a run-in with academic sexual harassment policy. While I will not here recount the gory details, I must refer to this experience in order to explain why I'm talking about this book." The "must" suggests that, although I do not want to, I find myself forced to "refer to this experience." "I must refer" but at least "I will not recount." Expressing a certain disgust for narratives of experience, I promise to spare the reader (or myself) "the gory details."

Anecdotal against its will, "*The Lecherous Professor*" would like to rise above the mire whence it originated. Trying to take as much distance as possible from the anecdotal, I am running scared. Running from the experiment in anecdotal theory I was pursuing less than two years earlier. Running for the safety of writing where the incidental roots of theory are relegated to their proper place— referred to briefly in the introduction but not recounted in the text proper.

I include "*The Lecherous Professor*" in this collection even though it represents a theorizing which would escape its anecdotal nature if it could. I include it precisely because I believe that the urge to escape the anecdotal is an inescapable part of anecdotal theory. To read this 1994 essay is to see theory struggling to overcome incident, and thus to understand better the stakes of anecdotal theory. No piece of writing in this collection is less anecdotal—less open to exploring the connections between its theorizing and lived experience. Yet, by the same token, no piece of writing in this collection is more anecdotal: no other theorizing was more compelled by incident.

The next essay in this collection was written just a month after "*The Lecherous Professor.*" If my first essay after the harassment incident wanted to drape itself in the mantle of scholarship, my second took on an utterly professional identity. Written for *Academe*, the magazine of the American Association of University Professors, "The Personal and the Professional" speaks as a professor to professors.

From the point of view of anecdotal theory, this essay has a lot of the same problems as the preceding one. Its introduction displays a similar reticence to speak of my personal experience: "This essay will outline what I have come to understand about the contradictions surrounding harassment policy in the academy. But since feminist epistemology has taught me the value of revealing the concrete conditions that produce knowledge, I feel I must speak, if only briefly, about my unfortunate personal experience." While we find here the same apologetic "must," this essay, unlike the previous one, specifies why I feel I must speak of my experience. This essay grounds that obligation in theory, in "feminist epistemology."

While "*The Lecherous Professor*" only referred to but did not recount my experience, this essay gives an account of the incident. That account is very controlled ("if only briefly") and thoroughly professional—hardly the "exorbitant" anecdotal writing I was doing at the beginning and end of the decade. While thus a poor example of the project, this essay does present some of the feminist argument for anecdotal theory: "Breaking down the barrier between the professional and the personal has been central in the feminist effort to expand the institution of knowledge to include what and how women know. . . . Feminist teachers saw the inclusion of the personal within the academic as a way to consider thoughts, responses, and insights which would not traditionally be recognized as knowledge."

The feminist argument for including the personal appears in this 1994 essay not for the purpose of justifying anecdotal theory but rather in order to counter the direction of sexual harassment policy. Because sexual harassment was framed as the intrusion of the personal into the professional, antiharassment activists were demanding we police the border between the professional and the personal. In order to question the feminist antiharassment demand for depersonalizing the academic, I juxtaposed it with the feminist epistemological claim for personalizing the academic. That juxtaposition not only delineates a really thorny theoretical problem in feminism but it also points toward connections between my resistance to sexual harassment policy and the project of anecdotal theory.

Writing the two 1994 essays did not slake my need to turn the harassment incident to theory. After writing the second essay, I decided to devote a whole book to explaining what I had been forced to learn. I wrote that book in 1995–96, called it *Feminist Accused of Sexual Harassment*. I didn't know what sort of book I was going to write, only that I felt compelled to write it. It turned out to be another experiment in anecdotal theory.

A lot of readers did not know what to make of the book's combining memoir with theory. Often faulted either for failing to give enough of the story or for failing to make a coherent, unified argument, the book was as disappointing to those who read it for memoir as to those who read it for theory.

The content of *Feminist Accused* was so flashy and high-profile—the topic so sensational, the position so controversial—that the question of its genre, its experiment in theoretical writing, was seldom noticed. It was a book whose topic could not help but overshadow its form. I think there is a connection between the book's argument and its form. Both challenge the divide between feeling and thought, between the passions of the thinking subject and her thinking. In the present book, I hope to make the epistemological stakes of the genre clearer by treating the practice (anecdotal theory) separately from the topic (the erotics of pedagogy). Nonetheless, the persistence of the latter topic in this book suggests that in my experience the two enterprises are so tightly entangled as to be separable only in theory.

A year after the publication of *Feminist Accused*, I wrote one more essay on sexual harassment policy. Although I no longer felt compelled to write about it, I had been, because of the book, invited to speak at a conference on the topic. The sense of professional legitimacy due to the invitation combined with the absence of personal urgency produced a tone unlike either the strident bitterness or the earnest professionalism of the 1994 texts. Rather than pointedly demonstrating my professionalism, I was by 1998 "Resisting Reasonableness."

This final essay in part 1 is one of the three pieces from the end of the decade. By 1998 I had returned to the experiment of theorizing through anecdote. This last essay on sexual harassment policy takes us to the end of "The Incident," to the place where we can (once again) take up "The Stories."

The story that gives rise to the theorizing in this essay does not, however, come from my own life; it is a story confided to me by someone as a result of her reading *Feminist Accused*. Whereas I had conceived of the book as beginning in story and proceeding to theory, in fact a number of readers responded to the book by telling or writing me their stories. Anecdotal theory, it turns out, is not a one-way street from story to theory, but a busy two-way traffic.

Basing its theory in a story confided to me, this essay is rooted not just in personal experience but in personal conversation. Many personal conversations are sites of anecdotal theorizing: friends and confidantes exchange stories from our lives and together try to make sense of them. "Resisting Reasonableness" attempts to bring this mode of intimate and intersubjective knowledge production into the academic realm of formal thinking and legitimated knowledge.

That last image sounds, however, too much like a one-way street again—as if we move from the personal to the professional and never go back the other way. In fact the exchange behind this essay did not take place in some strictly personal realm. This woman read my book, then sought me out to confide in me. When I decided to write about her story, I did so with her full knowledge and support. The personal conversation took place between these two publications—result of one, impetus to the other. This crossing back and forth between private and published exchange is not so uncommon. It is a circuit frequented by those of us avidly involved in both formal and intimate knowledge production—academics who become friends after reading each other's published scholarship, theorists who talk endlessly with intimates trying to make sense of our lives, whose conversations pass seamlessly back and forth between life stories and references to theoretical texts and concepts.

"Resisting Reasonableness" is one of two essays in this collection whose anecdotes come from someone else's life rather than my own. The other one is "The Teacher's Breasts," the first essay in part 1. The story in that essay was not confided to me personally; I read it in an academic publication, in another feminist scholar's attempt to theorize from an incident in her life. Like the stories people told me in response to reading *Feminist Accused,* my taking up and carrying on this other scholar's theorizing opens anecdotal theory beyond the closed circuit of individual life and mind. The opening and closing pieces of part 1 thus suggest a transindividual model for anecdotal theory (a model which will return as the broad network of disseminated sisterhood in the last essay of the collection).

Although "The Teacher's Breasts" is the first essay, I have saved it till last in this account of part 1. I deferred discussion of this 1992 essay because its place in "The Incident" is odd and seems hard to explain. "The Teacher's Breasts" was written before I was accused of sexual harassment. Later it became entangled in the incident. I wrote it in the summer of 1992 for a conference I was organizing on Pedagogy and the Personal for April 1993. By April, the students who had accused me of harassment and their supporters were protesting that conference. As I faced an audience aware of my accusation, reading a paper written before I was accused, I found the paper's bold playfulness around the erotics of pedagogy scary and dangerous. I was afraid my writing made me look guilty as charged.

I had, it turned out, written a paper about a bad feminist teacher, a teacher who sleeps with students, a teacher who responds to a student's request for feedback on his work by kissing and flirting with him. I had written a paper that featured a feminist sexual harasser, albeit a fictional one. These aspects which were so resonant with the case against me had not been central to my conception of the paper. But they are there, in a way that remains inescapable and embarrassing.

Although written in 1992, the moment when I was first engaged by the idea of theorizing from lived experience, "The Teacher's Breasts" was not intended as an attempt at anecdotal theory. It did not tell stories from my life; it was a critical reading of a theoretical text.

Actually, "The Teacher's Breasts" did have an anecdotal basis. The story behind this essay is in fact recounted in an essay in part 2, "Knot a Love Story," an essay written just a few months earlier. Whereas the essay in part 2 explicitly thinks through the incident from my own life, "The Teacher's Breasts" reads a story by someone else that resembles the story from my life and gives me a pretext for thinking through my story. The connection between these two essays leads me to wonder if a lot of critical reading, a lot of literary criticism isn't anecdotal in this same displaced way.

"The Teacher's Breasts" is in part 1 because it has a displaced, implicit, and murky relation to anecdotal theory. As part of "The Incident," it complicates the temporal relation between my writing and the harassment case. While the other essays in part 1 arose in response to the case, this one predated it, became entangled in it, and seems in retrospect to have predicted it.

By including "The Teacher's Breasts," I begin to see a more troubling relation between my life and my theoretical work. I prefer to think that life comes first and that theory is my way of mastering it through understanding. I prefer to theorize incident.

The fate of "The Teacher's Breasts," however, forces me to consider the possibility that sometimes theory precedes life, forces me to see my theorizing take on a life other than what I intended, forces me to watch my theory become itself an incident.

If the adjective "personal," elevated to noun status, has become a central focus for pedagogical theory, it is singularly due to something called "feminist teaching." Feminists teaching and feminists talking about teaching have not only challenged the exclusion of the personal from the academic but have gone so far as to insist that the proper measure of learning is personal. Even a cursory glance at feminist writing on pedagogy will yield a continual and widespread affirmation of "the personal"—as content, style, and method of pedagogy.

I have chosen to consider feminist pedagogy for the obvious reason that "the personal" is writ large there. But I'd like to take another look at feminist pedagogy for the perhaps more surprising reason that—despite all the validation, legitimation, affirmation, and celebration—in fact the personal remains a question there, a knotted, thorny, troubling question.

The editors of the best known collection of essays on feminist teaching tell us that one theme that recurs throughout the collection is, as they put it, "the transforming power of the personal as the subject and method of feminist education."[1] This 1985 anthology,

Gendered Subjects (regrettably now out of print in the United States), is a fair representation of the range and issues of feminist pedagogy, offering an opportunity to examine this "recurrent theme." The subtitle to *Gendered Subjects* is *The Dynamics of Feminist Teaching.* "Dynamics" may imply "transforming power," but it also suggests that this anthology is primarily concerned not with feminist curriculum, but with classroom dynamics and teacher-student relations. Feminist consideration of "the personal," in this volume as elsewhere, often refers to the inclusion of personal experience in class discussion and academic work. Although the phrase "Gendered Subjects" probably can include the gendering of subject matter, the title most likely implies that what characterizes "the dynamics of feminist teaching" is that students and teachers are themselves subject to gender and gendered subjectivities.

As might be expected, central to the volume is women teaching women. This relation is very much gendered, that is, thought according to models which characterize women precisely in contradistinction to men. These models tend to follow a strong psychoanalytic bent, particularly in the direction of the Chodorowian object-relations theory that had such currency in feminist academic discourse in the early 1980s. The teacher-student relation is again and again understood through analogy with the mother-daughter relation. The editors tell us that the collection originated in a paper entitled "The Politics of Nurturance," which they, along with three other colleagues, wrote in 1979.[2] "The Politics of Nurturance" is now the anthology's opening chapter, and nurturance is a key concept in *The Dynamics of Feminist Teaching.*

Although pedagogy between women both predominates and offers the book its theoretical paradigm, there are other gendered subjects in *Gendered Subjects.* Three of the essays are written by men.[3] Since the model for good or feminist teaching in this volume is a nurturance which does not transcend gender to something like "parenting" but remains tied to "mothering," these men are in a difficult position. All three reflect explicitly on the contradictions of feminist teaching by a man; in this context, they necessarily experience themselves as subject to gender; in this context, men teaching are aware that they cannot avoid the effects of gender upon their relations with students.

Although the *theoretical* pieces like "The Politics of Nurturance" are written as if all students were female,[4] in the volume's *experiential* tales of teaching, male students keep showing up. And making trouble.[5] Female and male teachers tend to respond to male students with fantasies not of nurturance but of discipline.

Each of these genderings of the pedagogical relation specifically and profoundly inflects the question of authority. The woman-to-woman paradigm shows the teacher giving up her authority and its association with distantiation in favor of blurring the boundaries between teachers and students. Maleness in either teacher or student affects this paradigmatic blurring of authority. The male teacher can't seem to get rid of his authority, particularly in the eyes of his female students, but he sure would like to. And the male student challenges the teacher's authority, particularly the female teacher's. However much the teacher might dream of divesting her- or himself of authority so as to get closer to the female student, she or he clearly does not want it taken away by the insubordinate male student. These structures are crude and schematic, but . . . as with most of the workings of gender and/or authority, the crude and schematic is usually all too apt.

Speaking of the crude and schematic: these genderings of the pedagogical relation likewise inflect the question of sex. The female/ female relation is explicitly celebrated as erotic.[6] It would seem, however, that "erotic" is not quite a synonym for "sexual" here, since the question of actual sexual relations is almost never posed. The single exception is the one out lesbian article which treats sexual relations, real and fantasized, between female teachers and students as a problem.[7] The contrast between this singular article— subtitled "My Life as the Only Lesbian Professor"—and the rest of the volume suggests that the unproblematic celebration of female/ female eroticism may itself be the site of unsuspected heterosexist presumption. The only lesbian essay aside, the female/female "erotic" shares in the general fluid boundaries of a maternalized femininity, a hyperfeminine gendering of sexuality.

In marked contrast with the rosy eroticism of all-female pedagogy, relations between male teachers and female students are sexualized as harassment. *Gendered Subjects*—true to its name—always explicitly genders sexual harassment: "sexual advances toward female students by male professors," as Adrienne Rich puts it.[8] And, as for male *students* . . . In the dynamics of gendered teaching, they pose a sexual question, if not a paradigmatic threat. They can neither be subsumed in the maternal desexualized erotic nor made to fit the sexual harassment case.

Around 1985, around the country, women's studies was expanding and/or being transformed into gender studies. The anthology *Gendered Subjects* partakes of that moment. Structures which applied to women alone are being expanded and/or transformed to include men as explicitly gendered. In this case, feminist teaching is no longer woman-to-woman, but gendered teacher/gendered student. The woman-to-woman model imagined feminist teaching as a safe space. When feminist teaching comes to mean the recognition that all pedagogical subjects are gendered, there is a real sense of loss in giving up the notion of that idealized safe space, but there is also, I would suggest, a substantial theoretical gain. *Gendered Subjects*, the book, entitles that gain, saying up front that feminist teaching is a dynamic between gendered subjects. Since, in fact, all teaching takes place between gendered subjects, feminist pedagogy can help us to see these gendered relations largely underrecognized in pedagogical theory.

■   ■   ■

I would like now to turn to a particularly dramatic scene of gendered pedagogy in *Gendered Subjects*. Helene Keyssar's contribution to the volume is an account of a feminist theater production course she taught. She gives her essay the ambiguous and evocative title "Staging the Feminist Classroom." Taking my cue from Keyssar's title, I read her essay as a representation of "*the* feminist classroom," and find connections between the story she tells of what happened in the classroom and the play the class actually stages.

Keyssar's pedagogical style and principles seem fairly typical of the volume. For example, explaining why, rather than assigning a script, she has the class as a whole choose the play they will perform, she tells us: "Although I knew that this would . . . minimize my control, I did so precisely to undermine my authority." She would like to "counter" her students' "perception" that she is the teacher and the director (110–11).

The script they choose is Susan Miller's "Cross Country," a play with a classic seventies feminist protagonist who leaves her marriage for a more risky and fulfilling autonomy. This particular feminist heroine, named Perry, not only leaves her husband but also, in the same self-liberating gesture, leaves her job as a college teacher. The simultaneity of these two gestures suggests that, like marriage, teaching constrains women.

Keyssar's pedagogical principles are straight out of the women's studies tradition, but—like many who promoted the move from women's to gender studies—she believes feminist teaching should not be restricted to women: "I made it clear that men were welcome in the course. . . . I wanted to make clear my own conviction that feminism was . . . not just . . . about women. . . . The presence of men in the class would make certain kinds of talk more problematic, but that kind of problematizing seemed valuable" (110). As expected, "the presence of men in the class" does indeed cause problems. The most dramatic moment in Keyssar's essay is an example of "that kind of problematizing" and provides a "valuable" lesson, for the class, the teacher, and then for the reader of *Gendered Subjects.* Keyssar's essay analyzes the moment for its theoretical implications and I would like here to continue that teaching, finding the incident particularly dense with implications for feminist pedagogy.

Keyssar specifically locates the scene within the larger drama of male students becoming explicitly and uncomfortably gendered in and by the feminist classroom: "The men in the class . . . were growing increasingly silent during class discussions . . . they showed a sense of being seen as the enemy" (117–18). Keyssar concludes her framing of the incident: "Their strongest feelings were the displeasure of exclusion from a group in which they wanted to be full members." This phrasing ("strongest feelings," "displeasure of exclusion," "in which they wanted to be full members") begins to suggest a scenario of frustrated penetration, as the students' maleness becomes increasingly salient.

Keyssar goes on: "These half-hidden tensions exploded unexpectedly in the context of a scene in which Perry asserts her power." This is a scene between Perry as teacher and a male student. Unlike Keyssar the feminist teacher who works to undermine her own authority, the protagonist (a feminist teacher from another genre) is "asserting her power." In the scene being rehearsed by Keyssar's class, Perry "assert[s] her power" by refusing to do her teacherly duties. She is behaving erratically, and, most important, refusing to take the term papers the students have just written for her. A crowd of students stands outside her office, shocked and confused by her unteacherly behavior. They choose a male student as their representative to go in and find out why she won't accept the papers. She tells him she likes his smile and insists he call her by her first name, then flippantly suggests that the students should rewrite and improve the papers she has not even looked at. He protests—"don't jack us off"— and she puts her arms around his neck and kisses him. "Now get the hell out of here," she says and kisses him again. And then once more, still telling him to go. The scene concludes with these stage directions: "He goes. But not without first touching her breasts."[9]

Perry here is a bad teacher. She is putting herself, her wishes and needs, before the needs of the students. Keyssar recounts this scene in detail, on her way to talking about an incident that happened during rehearsals. The scene produces interesting disruptions and reverberations when introduced into Keyssar's classroom, effects we will consider shortly. The scene likewise produces disruptive reverberations when rehearsed by Keyssar in the context of *Gendered Subjects*. Recounting this scene, Keyssar brings into the anthology, into the discourse on feminist teaching, something otherwise absent: the feminist as bad teacher.

As the heroine who stops being "good," stops catering to the needs of others, Perry comes from a long line of bad-girl feminists. Along with this "liberated woman," feminism has also always included a good-womanly image, championing heavily gendered superior female values. For example (and it always is the primary one): nurturance. These two images have jostled each other across the range of feminist thought and activities: sometimes in conflict, sometimes in alliance, less frequently in dialectical interaction. Most of the debates in feminist theory as well as many of the fights in feminist organization can, at least in part, be understood as playing out the confrontation between bad-girl and good-girl feminism.

Feminist pedagogy, however, has been an exception. In the discourse of feminist teaching, the bad girl has been at best an object, at worst invisible, but never a speaking subject. Although feminist pedagogy has sometimes promoted the bad-girl student, feminists as teachers have almost always spoken from the place of the good woman. Perhaps because teaching itself has been associated, since the common school movement of the early nineteenth century, with traditional "good" femininity, that is, with selfless, sexless nurturance. By retelling the scene in Perry's office, Keyssar casts the "bad girl" in the role of teacher on the stage of feminist pedagogy.

In bad-girl tradition, Perry pursues the sexual experimentation that two decades ago was sometimes mistaken for women's liberation. And one of her adventures, central to the play Keyssar's class chooses, yet never mentioned by Keyssar, is a love affair with a female student. In fact the term-paper-refusal, office-kiss scene occurs right after the student she is sleeping with leaves town in the middle of the term because the student can't cope with the affair. The bad-teacher scene anthologized in *Gendered Subjects* is linked to a worse-teacher scene. Bringing Susan Miller's sexualized teacher into the anthology, Keyssar provides a faint echo to Judith McDaniel, who, as the volume's "only lesbian professor," brings sexual trouble into the eroticized feminine space of nurturance.

Perry's affair with her student is never mentioned in *Gendered Subjects*. The bad-teacher scene that explicitly troubles Keyssar's feminist classroom is not woman-to-woman but female teacher/male student. And Keyssar focuses not on the bad teacher but on the problem student, the recalcitrant male student. Not the one in the play who touches the teacher's breasts, but the one in Keyssar's class who plays the one in the play. . . and who touches the teacher's breasts. . . wrong.

"Instead of approaching Perry hesitantly and literally touching her breasts, the man playing the student strode towards her and fiercely, with overt erotic impulse, grabbed and held each of her breasts" (118). I don't know what Keyssar's phrase "literally touching" literally means, but it suggests that when the script says "touching her breasts," the sense should be self-evident, "literal," not a matter for interpretation. And thus the interpretation by the so-called "man playing the student" would be particularly egregious. Keyssar tells it as if everyone else could see immediately how it should have been done, and the error thus could only be some sort of acting-out: "Unless he were extraordinarily violent or crazy, the young man would no more grab her breasts and caress them than he would disfigure a painting in a museum" (119).

I will return later to the analogy between the teacher's breasts and a painting in a museum. For now I want to follow the classroom drama of the problematic male student. At first merely unruly, when corrected he becomes obstinate: "The man playing the role of the male student insisted on the correctness of his initial interpretation, essentially on grounds that 'no man would do otherwise.' . . . Hours of talk seemed only to plunge us deeper into a mire of misunderstanding and, even when I violated one of my own cardinal rules and demonstrated the kind of touch most of us felt appropriate to the moment, the actor responded with a different, but even more eroticized, gesture than previously" (119).

Keyssar repeatedly refers to the culprit as "the man playing the student." He is, of course, also, among other things, the student playing the man in the scene, but she does not call him that. Her phrasing suggests that he is really a man but is only pretending to be a student. A real student would be too intimidated by a teacher to respond sexually. His "overtly erotic" gesture belies the role he is playing and reveals his true identity: "no man would do otherwise."

Given the setting of this confrontation in a general drama of male students in the feminist classroom, we might take this phrase "the man playing the student" to bespeak the contradiction posed by any male student, particularly for the female teacher. The contradiction, here played out around the question of sex, entails the question of authority. While the teacher has authority over the student, the *female* teacher has no authority over the man. What the student in the play does by touching the teacher's breasts, the student in the real classroom does by not accepting the teacher's interpretation of what would be appropriate student behavior.

Can a man be a student or, to the extent he is a man, is he only always playing a student, a fiction that is belied whenever he shows he is really a man? Is the student role itself, finally if only ever implicitly, gendered female? And maybe not just in feminist pedagogy?

"By reversing the rules of both student-teacher and male-female games," Keyssar writes, "Perry had made herself mysterious and impenetrable . . . the young man would no more grab her breasts . . . than he would disfigure a painting in a museum" (119). By being sexually aggressive, Perry is "reversing the rules of male-female games," making herself, so to speak, "impenetrable." But as for "student-teacher games": this scene of Perry "asserting her power" may be breaking the rules but is hardly a reversal of the teacher-student relation.

This sentence marks a point of confusion where "Staging the Feminist Classroom" is explicitly trying to think the gender relation ("male-female games") and the pedagogical relation ("student-teacher games") at the same time. The pairs are ordered so that student lines up with male, teacher with female. This is not the order of theoretical models of hierarchy, authority, and polarity, but rather comes from the actual relations at play, in the scene and in the classroom. Those relations are already, from the point of view of theoretical models, reversed. The encounter of female teacher and male student troubles any simple superimposition of these two sometimes analogous "games."

When the man plays the student and the woman plays teacher, gender rules may be reversed, but pedagogical rules are broken. Perry breaks those rules by being seductive and irresponsible toward her student. She has already broken what McDaniel in *Gen-*

dered Subjects calls "Rule Number One: teachers do not become [sexually] involved with students" (133). And, in the context of Perry's unruly behavior, Keyssar too, in her encounter with the stubbornly male-gendered student, finds herself breaking rules: "I violated one of my own cardinal rules and demonstrated the kind of touch most of us felt appropriate."

Whereas McDaniel's Rule Number One explicitly concerns sex, Keyssar's "cardinal rule" concerns authority. Presumably it forbids her from showing students what to do, rather than letting them figure it out, in keeping with her general style of teaching and directing. Yet, faced with a man in place of a student, she finds herself assuming the position of authority she has worked so hard to avoid. Keyssar describes Perry's scene with the male student as "asserting her power," and, although we might want to question that characterization of Perry, the phrase does very aptly describe Keyssar's response to *her* male student. Perry and Keyssar, in very different ways, both end up treating the male student as a man rather than a student: Perry by flirting rather than caring, Keyssar by trying to overcome rather than empower.

The man playing a student drives Keyssar to lay bare the authority that as a feminist teacher she has been underplaying. To her consternation, her authority does not put him in his place as a student: "Even when I violated one of my own cardinal rules . . . the actor responded with a[n] . . . even more eroticized gesture." To Keyssar's surprise, asserting her authority makes the male student more not less recalcitrant, and more not less sexual.

Keyssar gradually comes to understand that "he could not project anything but aggression in response to a woman's exhibition of power" (119). The conflict is resolved when the feminist class recognizes the male student's gender:

> We assumed . . . that the man could leap into the role of the sexually exploited person—but everything in his experience refuted the possibility of such a role for a man. . . . All of our attempts to "enlighten" the male actor had been based on accounts by women of incidents in which men in positions of

power had made sexual approaches to them. . . . We had asked the actor to think of himself in that moment as a woman, but . . . he had to conjure up a world in which women had power and used it. . . . Once we were able to admit the complexity of his task, the actor was freed to attempt affable imitation of what he thought we wanted, and that, in the end, was better than where we had begun. (119–20)

"In the end . . . better than where we had begun": the "kind of problematizing" produced by "the presence of men in the class" proves "valuable" as the incident ends happily. They were trying to fit the man into a women's studies model—"we had asked the actor to think of himself . . . as a woman"—but are forced to move beyond that model to a gendered pedagogy. Once they recognize that he is a man, he is able to "play" a student.

Despite this neat resolution of the conflict, a couple of questions about the incident remain, questions that are central for feminist pedagogy, at least as represented in this 1985 anthology grappling with feminist teaching beyond the all-feminine classroom. The first question involves pronouns, identities, individuals, and collectives; the second will return us to the teacher's breasts.

In the passage just quoted, you might have noticed that Keyssar consistently uses a first person plural pronoun. The conflict is represented as between the class as a whole ("we") and the man: "he" is the problem, the singular which must be resolved back into the ensemble.[10] At the moment that she breaks her cardinal rule, however, she uses a first person singular pronoun. His obstinate singularity forces hers, pushes her into the role of teacher, and breaks the illusion that she is just part of the ensemble.

This staging of the classroom as "we" vs. "he" resonates with Keyssar's interpretation of the teacher-student scene in the play. Although otherwise quite complete, her account of the scene leaves one significant detail out. Miller's script tells us that the student entering Perry's office is the elected representative of the crowd of students outside the door. In the play, it is the male student who can oppose the teacher with a "we." Keyssar never mentions his representative status, introducing him only as "one male student who assertively enters her office," thus constructing him as different from the rest of the students, positioning him as she does the student in her class. The juxtaposition of the scene in Perry's office and the drama in Keyssar's classroom poses the question: who can speak for the class and who stands apart from the pedagogical "we," the male student or the female teacher? Keyssar's interpretation tends toward embodying difference in the male student.

I see here the work of the Chodorowian model of gender that subtends the volume as a whole. In that model, individuation is itself gendered male. Although the many feminist theorists who have contributed to the gendering of distinction vs. togetherness undoubtedly intended to be descriptive, gendered descriptions seem unable to avoid powerful prescriptive effect.

The maternalized model of femininity might also be at work in Keyssar's interpretation of the teacher's breasts. In order to demonstrate the correct approach, Keyssar has recourse to a surprising analogy: "The young man would no more grab her breasts and caress them than he would disfigure a painting in a museum. He might, however, fleetingly touch a painting—or a breast—to test its reality and to determine limits" (119). What she first refers to as a literal touch is here, by means of the figure of the painting, specified as "fleeting." And as Keyssar is finally able, by analogy, to articulate her interpretation, the breasts become singular: "fleetingly touch a painting—or *a* breast" (my emphasis).

As Keyssar imagines it, the only appropriate way to touch the teacher's breast*s* is to touch the teacher's *breast*. The problem is that Miller's script specifies the plural. Not only is it much harder to imagine a fleeting touch of *both* breasts but, beyond the problem of physical interpretation, it seems to me that the difference between breast and breasts is precisely the difference between a symbolic and a sexual interpretation. The difference between the breast and the breasts might function like the infamous phallus/penis relation.[11]

In the context of feminist pedagogy, it might also signify the difference between the good teacher and the bad. There is one other breast in *Gendered Subjects,* precisely one and not two. "The Politics of Nurturance" suggests that the woman teacher "purveys the maternal breast" (16). The breast—singular, symbolic, and maternal—is precisely the imaginary organ of nurturance, what the good feminist teacher proffers to her daughter-students. Refusing to nurture, Perry the bad sexual teacher brings into the discourse of feminist pedagogy not the breast, which is already appropriately there, but the breasts.

Like a painting in a museum, the breast is idealized, decontextualized, and removed from history. It belongs to the infantile misperception of the mother, when the infant takes the breast for part of his body, before he perceives the mother as a separate person. The pre-Oedipal fantasies that underpin the teacher as nurturing mother lead teachers like Keyssar to submerge her subjectivity in the cozy "we" of the feminist classroom.

Gendered Subjects repeatedly and invaluably stages the confrontation of this dream of the feminist classroom with the question of gender. The incident I have considered is no doubt the most dramatic example but is otherwise not unrepresentative. The bad-girl feminist teacher and the male student who rubs his teacher the wrong way disrupt the idyllic hyperfeminine space of a gender-appropriate feminist classroom.

Keyssar states that she welcomes men into the feminist classroom, knowing they will disrupt the feminine, knowing they will cause problems, but wagering that the "problematizing" will be valuable. I share Keyssar's belief in the value of that disruption. I see it as part of a theoretical move frequently staged in this anthology. Beginning with a model of maternal pedagogy, *Gendered Subjects* repeatedly calls that model into question—sometimes theoretically, sometimes anecdotally, sometimes unwittingly, sometimes directly. A maternal pedagogy might appear utopian but it is also subject to traditionally gendered prescription. While feminist teaching based in appropriate feminine behavior has been implicitly defined by gender, feminist pedagogy can teach us to analyze the effects of gender in our pedagogical practice rather than just acting them out.

The Lecherous Professor, written by Billie Wright Dziech and Linda Weiner, was published in 1984 by Beacon Press and, in a second edition, in 1990 by the University of Illinois Press. With its university press second edition, *The Lecherous Professor* became recognizable as the first scholarly book exclusively focused on what the book's subtitle calls *Sexual Harassment on Campus*. Interested in that very subject—and what is more, finding myself an interested party in the subject—I thought to order the book, but I must confess that what really moved me to read it was the novelistic title, whose sensationalism I wanted to transmit by putting it in the title of my essay.

Before I begin my commentary on Dziech and Weiner's *Lecherous Professor*, I feel it quite necessary to consider if, how, and why this book is worth devoting time and attention to. My professional formation included internalizing the lesson that the only texts worth commentary, particularly if the commentary were critique, are texts that have power for the critic. In other words, it is not worth expending one's ingenuity to demonstrate that a text you think is dumb is, in fact, dumb. I have carried this lesson fervently to my students, trying to teach them the difference between valuable critique and dismissiveness. And as I prepared to write about this book, I worried I might be—or the reader might think I was— indeed wasting our time suggesting that a book my reader would probably never consider reading is not worthwhile.

In fact, my aim is precisely to suggest the value of understanding what is going on in this academic book about sex in the institution of knowledge. The problem is that I want to talk at length and in detail about a book that I myself don't think very highly of, a book that to my mind thinks neither clearly nor subtly. Yet, bound and determined to talk about this book, I am forced to rethink one of the central lessons of my intellectual formation.

But (let me be clear in case any of my students should ever read these words) "rethink" here means not recant but reconceptualize. While I feel as strongly as ever that the only texts worth critique are "texts that have power for the critic," I have been brought to reconsider what "power" means in that criterion. In my professional formation—both what my teachers did for me and what I do for my students—I have always understood that word to mean intellectual power, something like good ideas, or subtle thinking, or trenchant formulations. This is the centrally recognized form of power in the discipline where I work—let's still call it "theory." Dziech and Weiner's book has a very different sort of power, one my teaching has encouraged me to disdain.

In the last two years I have had a run-in with academic sexual harassment policy. While I will not here recount the gory details, I must refer to this experience in order to explain why I'm talking about this book.[1] In this last while, I've learned the hard way about the politics of deconstructive intervention. For the record, I need to say that I never sexually harassed anyone, never made (and this is the standard definition) "unwelcome sexual advances" to anyone. But (and this is to the point of what I have to say here) I publicly located myself precisely at what I considered to be the most glaring point of contradiction in the university's sexual policy. I imagined that as a woman and a recognized feminist I could intervene to expose a troubling and misguided contradiction in the policy, but those who enforce the policy had their own interpretive methodology which determined me to be in contradiction with, that is, in violation of, the policy.

I thought I knew all about sexual harassment because I understood its most sophisticated theoretical articulations; I felt superior to my university's policy because I'm a feminist theorist and it was based in muddled feminist theory. I have learned how very naive my sophisticated disdain was. I'm sure only an intellectual would be so dumb as to think herself not subject to a regulation because she could see how easily it deconstructed itself.

Using the disciplinary criterion of intellectual power, I had read only a restricted slice of feminist theory. As a result, I had not realized the pervasiveness of the wrongheaded and confused feminist theory reflected in university policy. While the people I read and the people who read me were busy formulating ever more sophisticated feminist conceptions of sex, another group of feminists was establishing their theorization of sex as policy governing the very academy where "we" were doing cutting-edge feminist theory.

The Lecherous Professor is representative of this other feminist theory. I think it worthy of critique because it partakes in the power to shape and instill institutional policy. But I turn our attention to this text in particular because it does not belong directly to the genre of policy. *The Lecherous Professor* is not only published by a university press but is in fact a scholarly book.

In the conclusion, the authors write: "Sophisticated inquiry is what higher education does better than any other institution. . . . But forced to deal with sexual harassment, higher education has behaved as if it is incapable of sophisticated inquiry and must rely instead on second-grade approaches. . . . It is possible to apply academe's own rigorous standards of inquiry to sexual harassment. The very act of analyzing the problem should lead naturally to an intellectual and psychological breakthrough for institutions, administrators, faculty, and students" (185–86).

I recognize Dziech and Weiner as sister workers in the production of knowledge. I share deeply this belief in the value and appropriateness of "sophisticated inquiry" and rigorous analysis. In fact, my problem with academic sexual policy is precisely that it isn't academic enough, that it has not been formulated according to "academe's own rigorous standards of inquiry," that the "sophisticated inquiry" prized by the university has not sufficiently contributed to developing the very policies which now regulate our inquiry.

In their introduction, the authors invite us to take *The Lecherous Professor* as a scholarly, and even theoretical, contribution to the collective effort to produce knowledge about sexual harassment: "We hope our theories will be analyzed, tested and refined through continued research and analysis so we might all acquire fuller understanding of sexual harassment" (5). I propose here to take them at their word (although my own "research methods" might not be the social scientific methodology they had in mind). By reading their book, I hope here to take up again my project of intervening in the discourse on sexual harassment. This time around, rather than a flashy but unglossed performance of civil disobedience, I will instead attempt to spell out a deconstruction of the theorizing that underwrites the policies. By thus operating within a genre easier to recognize as scholarly, I hope not only to avoid certain kinds of trouble but, ultimately, to make a more effective intervention.

■   ■   ■

Upon first reading Dziech and Weiner, I was struck by their use of the metaphor of the closet. An example from the first chapter: "Despite all the visibility and public discussion of students' rights and women's concerns on campus, sexual harassment remained in the closet" (11). Two examples from the last chapter: "The fact is that the distinctions between harassers and their peers are very definite. There are few closet harassers" (179); and "so many academicians . . . have allowed harassment to become a private rather than a professional consideration. . . . Sexual harassment has been a titillating closet issue" (185). The most recent example is from the preface to the 1990 second edition: "Sexual harassment has not disappeared from our campuses and . . . development of policies and programs has not eliminated the problem—and perhaps never will. But at least the issue is out of the closet and in the public consciousness" (xv).

I cannot read the closet metaphor without thinking of homosexuality. Yet that would suggest some connection between homosexuality and harassment. Of course, both have been secrets that, like other secrets, especially sexual ones, the contemporary ethos deems it healthy to bring out into the light of day ("out of the closet and in[to] the public consciousness"). While the association is thus logical, it nonetheless presents a problem: whereas contemporary liberal opinion concurs that harassment is perversion, that is, bad sexuality, liberals currently try to avoid the notion that homosexuality is perversion. This makes the use of the closet metaphor here seem, at least, unfortunate. I did not want to jump to the conclusion of homophobia, but I did find it surprising that two feminist writers of the 1980s could use the metaphor of the closet apparently without considering its homosexual connotations.

Dziech and Weiner explicitly chose not to deal with homosexuality by restricting their study to heterosexual harassment, specifically to male professors harassing female students. This restriction seems quite justifiable because that form of harassment not only provides the vast majority of cases (90 percent, we were told at a department workshop)[2] but is unquestionably the paradigmatic form. However reasonable the decision, the language they use while explaining their choice does trouble me: "Early in our investigation, we decided to treat only the subject of sexual harassment of women students by male professors. This is not to deny that there are incidents of female professors harassing male students or homosexuals harassing collegians" (3).

Now, to be sure, it is likely that the authors were trying to be elegant and economical by avoiding the long-winded and repetitive recital of all four possible gender configurations for student-teacher harassment, by condensing both same-sex possibilities into one phrase. (Although we might also want to note that it is not infrequently the case that the manifest goal of stylistic grace is an effective carrier for latent chunks of crudely inappropriate ideology.)[3] Yet I have seen more felicitous and less irregular solutions to this same stylistic dilemma. However innocent the authors' intentions, the phrase "homosexuals harassing collegians" demands commentary.

Whereas the heterosexual harassers (male and female) would certainly be condemned for their behavior, in Dziech and Weiner's formulation they nonetheless retain their identities as "professors." But the harassing homosexuals have nothing but a sexual identity. On the other hand, calling the victims "collegians" foregrounds the relation to the institution.[4] Whereas in both the heterosexual variations listed perpetrator and victim are given parallel structure, with each having both an institutional and a gender identity, in the homosexual version, the perpetrator has only a sexual identity and the innocent victim is identified only with the institution. The phrase thus construes the harassing homosexual as outside the institution while emphasizing the victim as an insider, presenting us with the vintage conservative moral scenario of outsiders invading and polluting a pure and innocent interior.

So, a piece of homophobia lies exposed in *The Lecherous Professor*. As regrettable or distasteful as this lapse may be, it need not entirely compromise the book. It would be impractically idealistic to refuse to benefit from the work of anyone who manifested any prejudices. The real question is whether the homophobia is centrally involved with the book's project, and beyond that (and more to the point of our concerns), whether homophobia is structurally intricated with the general theorization of sexual harassment in which this book participates.

I am not the only one to notice a connection between homophobia and the discourse around sexual harassment. Sociologist Barry Dank, founder of Consenting Academics for Sexual Equity, writes: "We know that the sorts of stereotypical imagery that the contemporary campus banning advocates apply to professor-student relationships is the same sort of rhetoric that traditional homophobics have applied to gay men."[5] Actually, Dank is here referring not to literal homophobia in contemporary antiharassment discourse but to the use of the rhetoric of homophobia. His comment does not connect so much to the direct appearance of homophobia in *The Lecherous Professor* ("homosexuals harassing collegians"), although it reminds me rather more of my worries about the analogy suggested by the closet metaphor. But it applies most directly to what is unquestionably the single most dubious theoretical construction in Dziech and Weiner's book.

The fifth chapter itself bears the book's title, "The Lecherous Professor," suggesting that this chapter is in some way central. The subtitle of this chapter is "A Portrait of the Artist." I don't know what to make of the literary allusion, nor of the notion that harassment is an art,[6] but I can tell you that this chapter sets about to sketch a psychological profile of the harassing professor. And although three psychological motivations for such behavior are considered, a quite disproportionate amount of time is devoted to the first hypothesis—"arrested adolescent development" (138).

Now, while much of Dziech and Weiner's book is careful, insightful, and well-taken, the procedure in the fifth chapter is extremely questionable. Here is the explanation of their method: "There is . . . no means to gather . . . the enormous retrospective data necessary to establish an image of a prototypic sexual harasser. What *can* be examined are some relevant questions about contemporary male professors. . . . Are there knowable similarities in the developmental cycles of a significant number of men who choose the academic profession?" (125). In order to explain the behavior of harassers, the authors examine the collective motivation of professors. Dziech and Weiner are, to be sure, careful to state that the majority of male professors are not harassers. Because of the specific focus of the book, *The Lecherous Professor* neglects to mention that outside the academy are plenty of sexual harassers who are not professors, yet it uses differences between professors and other men to explain harassment. Most professors are not lechers; most lechers are not professors; yet "The Lecherous Professor" assumes it can determine the psychology of harassers by looking at the psychology of male professors in general.

In her note to the second edition, Dziech discusses a problem in the reception of the first edition: "Too many assume that it's a sweeping indictment of all males in the profession instead of an attempt to differentiate the offenders . . . from the vast majority of male academicians" (xvii). The syllogism in the chapter "The Lecherous Professor" is no doubt responsible for the widespread "mistaken" assumption Dziech here decries. But as illogical as the procedure in the fifth chapter is, what is most troubling about it, to my mind, is the fact that this arbitrary and ill-founded move makes possible the construction of the harasser as a case of "arrested adolescent development," which is to say, it produces a psychological diagnosis which just happens to be identical to the pathologizing of homosexuality which dominated most of the last century.

On the way to formulating this arrested adolescent diagnosis, the fifth chapter remarks in passing: "Whatever the language, almost all developmental theories stress the importance of adolescence as the time during which one . . . develops satisfying relationships with peers of the same sex, forms adequate heterosexual relationships, and lays the foundation for a career choice" (127). Among the tasks of adolescence, apparently accepted as such by Dziech and Weiner, is the forming of "adequate heterosexual relationships." The complacent heterosexism revealed here, while perhaps less extreme, is ultimately more disturbing than the book's sporadic homophobia.

I am here making the somewhat arbitrary distinction between heterosexism and homophobia, knowing full well not only their necessary entanglement but the impossibility of actually drawing a line between them. I want nonetheless to employ the two terms to signal two different levels of phenomena. I am using homophobia to designate the extreme, dramatic, and egregious pathologizing of homosexuality that can appear in antiharassment discourse. I'm reserving heterosexism for the less flagrant and more systemic invisibility of any sexuality that is not heterosexual, for the unstated founding assumption that sexuality is synonymous with heterosexuality.

My reading of *The Lecherous Professor* has turned up an instance or more of homophobia. While both shocking and offensive, it seems nonetheless contingent. Although *this* book may be homophobic, certainly other texts which share its notion of sexual harassment are free of these unseemly manifestations. Yet, while it may be formulated without homophobia, the conceptualization of sexual harassment that Dziech and Weiner share with a broad spectrum of writers and activists is systemically heterosexist. The heterosexism is ultimately more troubling than the homophobia because, while the latter can be written off to a weak book, the former underpins a strong movement.

Although I am here making a case for heterosexism's greater significance, before I move on to my analysis of heterosexism, I want to explain why I have devoted so much time to homophobia. Not least of my reasons is the greater sensationalism of homophobia, the shock and fascinating horror of its crudity. I do not want to dismiss the sensational, for it was what drew my attention. Were it not for the phrase "homosexuals harassing collegians," I would not have thought to pursue the question of heterosexism in the formulation of sexual harassment. So, while the narrative of this essay moves toward heterosexism as the more serious category for this critique, it is in fact the very entanglement between heterosexism and homophobia that makes this analysis possible.

Central to heterosexism is the conflation of, on the one hand, sex and, on the other hand, sex. The division of human beings into sexes, often called opposite sexes, is understood to be synonymous with sex, meaning sexuality, sexual behavior, sexual attraction. The commonplace, magnetic formulation "opposites attract" is understood to express the self-evident equation between the opposite sex and sexuality. It is this profound conflation between sex and sex that underlies a central deformation of the notion of sexual harassment.

A feminist academic leading a university workshop on sexual harassment, contemptuous of professorial worry that students might misconstrue his behavior, dismisses the concern as obstructionist quibbling and confidently announces: "Come on. We know what sex is." I repeat this smug pronouncement here because I imagine that its certitude will arouse protest on behalf of current notions of the complexity and ambiguity of both gendering and sexuality. It's a cheap shot and not directly my point here. Rather, my point is that, even if we bracket all those sophisticated notions, in fact "we" do not even know what the word "sex" refers to in sexual harassment. Contrary to popular belief, the word "sexual" in the phrase "sexual harassment" does not mean that the harassment is sexual (i.e., lascivious), but rather harassment *on the basis of sex.*[7]

It is, to be sure, quite understandable that the meaning of "sexual harassment" should be so widely mistaken. Standard definitions typically include both senses of the word "sex," making it all the more likely they will be conflated. For example, the definition from the U.S. Office of Civil Rights states that "sexual harassment consists of . . . conduct of a sexual nature, imposed on the basis of sex . . . that . . . conditions the provision of . . . benefits."[8] Not only is it hard to tell if what makes this harassment "sexual" is the "sexual nature" of the conduct or the "basis of sex" on which it is imposed, but it is difficult simply to keep in mind that the two are not the same.

Sexual harassment was conceptualized by feminists in the late 1970s. "Lin Farley's [1978 book] *Sexual Shakedown* and Catherine MacKinnon's [1979 book] *Sexual Harassment of Working Women* treated sexual harassment as a type of sex discrimination . . . rather than a sexual issue. Court cases, publications, and policy-makers refined and maintained that position" (*Lecherous Professor*, 19). In 1980 the U.S. Equal Employment Opportunity Commission amended its "Guidelines on Discrimination Because of Sex" by adding the category of sexual harassment, stating: "Harassment on the basis of sex is a violation of Section 703 of Title VII."[9] Sexual harassment became illegal because it was recognized as an instance of "discrimination because of sex." This sense of sexual harassment is accurately represented by Dziech and Weiner. Weiner's note to the second edition is particularly pithy on this topic: "Sexual harassment is not about sex, it's about sexism" (xxv).

Despite the clarity of this statement and despite Dziech and Weiner's careful transmission of the standard working definitions of sexual harassment, entitling their book *The Lecherous Professor* certainly reinforces the idea that sexual harassment is about sex, not sexism. This focus on lechery rather than sexism, which goes directly counter to their knowledge of the meaning and history of the concept, is in fact typical of a general slippage in the understanding of sexual harassment. I am trying to suggest here that what underlies this slippage must be recognized as absolutely the most profound and widespread heterosexism.

There is good reason indeed for a heterosexist conceptualization of sexual harassment—after all, sexual harassment is *itself* paradigmatically heterosexist. Consider, for example, the following proposition reported in *The Lecherous Professor*: a male professor walks up to a female student unhappy with her grade and says, " 'There's one option I can give to you that I can't give to the males in the class. Sex?' " (94). When a male professor looks at a female student and presumes his relation to her is sexual, he is merely putting into explicit practice the fundamental assumption of heterosexism: that sexuality and relations between the sexes are synonymous. The presumption that any relation to the opposite sex is sexual necessarily follows from that assumption. Paradigmatic sexual harassment is literally the enactment of a conflation between the two senses of sex.

By choosing to consider only the paradigmatic form of harassment (male professors harassing female students), Dziech and Weiner avoid confronting the difference between lechery and sex discrimination. What they all too quickly dismiss behind the homophobic facade of "homosexuals harassing collegians" might just be the necessity to think about "conduct of a sexual nature" which is not "imposed on the basis of sex."

For example, consider the blithely heterosexist, and otherwise unreal, suppositions behind statements such as: "Male faculty members do not compliment male students on their bodies or clothing, and there is really no reason they must do so with women" (180). Even were we to grant the assumption that classic homophobic male teachers "do not compliment male students on their clothing," we immediately see the difficulty of moving this "guideline" beyond the paradigmatic case. Just imagine the parallel statement: "Female faculty members do not compliment female students on their clothing." Recognizing that a compliment on clothing can indeed be a "sexual advance," determining when it is becomes much more complicated once we give up our confidence that "we know what sex is," that the sexual is located in relations between the sexes.

We must resist the heterosexist understanding of sexual harassment, not merely for the liberal reason that it unwittingly contributes to the invisibility of people and practices that are not heterosexual. Rather for the more intrinsic reason that, by maintaining the heterosexist conflation at the heart of antiharassment discourse, we are not only guilty of the same failing as the harasser himself (which is embarrassing enough) but are unintentionally reinforcing the mindset which produces sexual harassment. What causes someone to assume his relation to the opposite sex is sexual is in fact not merely sexism but heterosexism.

In order to combat sexual harassment, we must disrupt rather than subscribe to this ambient heterosexism. Whereas the harasser's heterosexism leads him to discriminate by being sexual, the anti-harasser's heterosexism leads her to assume that all sexuality is discriminatory. In both cases no distinction is made between sexuality and the relation between the sexes. While the harasser is, in one and the same act, sexist and sexual, precisely *because* he is, we must be able to distinguish sexuality and sexism. And we must always bear in mind that harassment is despicable and illegal, not because it is sexual, but because it is sexist.

■ ■ ■

The Lecherous Professor recognizes that harassment is sex discrimination but at the same time it also muddles that recognition in the tendency toward sensationalism so well exemplified by the title. One might say that the 1984 book cannot decide whether it's about sex . . . or about sex. By the 1990 second edition, these two entangled meanings are beginning to separate.

Nothing in the first edition marked any division between the two coauthors. In the preface to the second edition, however, Dziech and Weiner apprise us that "as the following authors' notes indicate, [the two of them] do not always share a common approach to the issue" (xv). As we read their separate author's notes in the second edition, only one issue distinguishes them, and, although they say that they are nevertheless "in agreement on the most crucial points," I would contend that the one issue that separates them is *absolutely* crucial to the interpretation of sexual harassment.

Billie Wright Dziech tells us in her author's note that she has "retain[ed her] original conviction that genuine change can occur only when [sexual harassment] is approached as a professional rather than a gender issue" (xviii). I want to query this "conviction" that sexual harassment should be "approached as a professional rather than a gender issue." How can "discrimination on the basis of sex" *not* be a gender issue?

As if in direct response to Dziech's conviction, Linda Weiner in her author's note retorts: "We should not be ashamed to call sexual harassment a women's issue. We should abandon strategies that hope to gain more support by casting sexual harassment . . . as gender-free. . . . It *is* a women's issue, and declaring it androgynous only disguises its true nature" (xxix). Although I'm not exactly sure what Weiner means here by "androgynous" and I'm generally uncomfortable with the idea of "true nature," I wholeheartedly concur that if we cut sexual harassment free from gender, we will deform it beyond recognition, transforming it into something quite other than its original feminist formulation; without gender, sexual harassment can no longer be a type of sex discrimination.

Reading this implicit debate in the 1990 author's notes, I feel my mixed response to the book splitting into sympathy for one author, antipathy for the other. Knowing full well that they produced this book together and that I cannot reasonably attribute everything I like to one and everything I don't to the other, I nevertheless want to use the articulated difference between these two coauthors to represent a bifurcation in feminist antiharassment discourse. At a certain moment in the early 1980s they were able to work together seamlessly. By 1990 the difference becomes explicit. I can see a time—we might be there already—when it will be necessary to choose between them. As I conclude my paper by discussing the differences between Dziech and Weiner, I hope you can hear this not primarily as a preference between individuals but, more importantly for my purposes, as an allegory, contrasting two possible directions for the discourse on sexual harassment.

Weiner's individual statement begins: "Sexual harassment has been a whetstone for my feminism, giving it a keener, more radical edge" (xxv). Weiner's work against sexual harassment has sharpened her feminist commitment; for her, the battle against harassment is part of the larger feminist struggle. Weiner is the author who succinctly states: "Sexual harassment is not about sex, it's about sexism" (xxv). Given the focus of the present essay, it is worth remarking that Weiner's Note to the second edition contains the only instance in the book of the word "homophobia" (xxvii). Although she uses the term in the most predictable obligatory list along with "racism" and "classism," what would in many contexts be an unremarkable feminist gesture here at least demonstrates a passing familiarity with homophobia as a necessary category for feminist thinking in the nineties. In a context as generally hetero-sexist as *The Lecherous Professor,* we might take even this superficial concern as a good sign.

Weiner's coauthor, on the other hand, seems to be pursuing quite another path. In December 1993, Dziech published an opinion piece on sexual harassment in *The Chronicle of Higher Education*; she has clearly "retained" her "conviction" that sexual harassment can be separated from gender. But now she explicitly states the implicit corollary, that it can be separated from feminism. The opinion piece is devoted to the issues surrounding sexual harassment in the present moment, in what Dziech calls a "new phase of the debate":

> To understand this new phase of the debate, we should be-gin by recognizing that the issue of sexual harassment is sepa-rable from feminist philosophy. It is impossible to overestimate the contribution that feminists made in bringing the problems of harassment to the attention of society. But their very suc-cess insured that more diverse groups would eventually recog-nize the legitimacy of the issue and begin to explain it in their own ways.
>
> That transition is already under way, and whatever the future of feminism, sexual harassment is a subject that now stands on its own. . . . Students . . . have developed their own ways of explaining it. Such students frequently see harassment as a viola-tion of morality. I suspect that eventually the political right, which originally conceded the issue to the left, will take a second look and embrace protections against sexual harassment as part of its agenda for a return to traditional values.[10]

This vision of co-optation into the return to traditional values is exactly what frightens me about the heterosexist tendencies within antiharassment discourse. Although I will try to avoid leaping to the conclusion that Dziech sides with the right here, I am chilled by her dispassionate, "objective tone" as she describes this eventuality. Whatever her opinion of this possible turn of affairs, her sense that this reinterpretation of sexual harassment is concomitant with the issue becoming separate from feminism is absolutely to the point.

"Whatever the future of feminism, sexual harassment is a subject that now stands on its own," asserts Dziech, sounding to my ears all too proud of this independence, perhaps taking it as a sign that the battle against sexual harassment has come of age (the "new phase"). I hear this announcement as a wake-up call. The phrase "whatever the future of feminism" alarms me because I care much, much more about the future of feminism than about a single-issue campaign against sexual harassment. When the fight against harassment is no longer a struggle against sexism but a moral crusade against sexuality, it is all too likely to be not just nonfeminist, not just heterosexist but "part of [the right's] agenda for a return to traditional values," which is to say, quite pointedly antifeminist.

For more than two decades, I have been working as a feminist in the academy. In the early seventies, as an undergraduate, I served on the advisory committee for the women's studies program just being established at Cornell University. I earned my doctorate in the mid-seventies, writing a feminist dissertation. At Miami University in the early eighties, I taught the capstone seminar for women's studies seniors, helping them do original feminist research in their respective majors. In the mid-eighties I was hired to set up a women's studies program at Rice University, which for regional as well as other reasons was very late in doing so. During my time at Rice, I got a solid undergraduate women's studies curriculum off the ground and organized a range of faculty across the humanities and social sciences into the faculty feminist research group. In 1990 I left Rice for the University of Wisconsin, Milwaukee, which had hired me to teach feminist theory for the large number of graduate students doing feminist work in the Department of English and Comparative Literature. In late 1992, I was informed that two women, feminist graduate students, had filed complaints of sexual harassment against me.

This came as quite a shock. Sexual harassment, conceptualized by feminist theorists, is part of the larger pattern of discrimination against women; sexual harassment is a way men obstruct women from doing work. University policies against sexual harassment aim to ensure that women have as much chance as men to pursue knowledge. My own work has likewise been part of the larger feminist effort to truly open the university to women. While coeducation allows women to join men in men's pursuit of knowledge, the movement for women's studies works to bring about an academy that includes what women know. I have administered, taught, researched, and written as part of this movement to include women fully as knowers within the institution of knowledge—yet, after two decades, I found myself accused precisely of depriving women of the opportunity to pursue knowledge. The irony could not have been sharper.

My accusers claimed the contradiction was mine: while I pretended to be a feminist, to support women's pursuit of knowledge, in reality, just like the proverbial male pig professor, I did not take these women seriously as students. While I too believe this case exposes contradiction, I don't believe the contradiction is mine. The situation in which I found myself was not merely a personal irony but rather, I think, brings to light incongruities in the formulation and application of sexual harassment policy.

This essay will outline what I have come to understand about the contradictions surrounding harassment policy in the academy. But since feminist epistemology has taught me the value of revealing the concrete conditions that produce knowledge, I feel I must speak, if only briefly, about my unfortunate personal experience. The university's Office of Affirmative Action conducted a lengthy and thorough investigation, which looked into not only the two complaints but also my relations with students in general. No evidence whatsoever, either of discrimination or of harassment, was found. I had not attempted to gain sexual favors from students, had always judged students according to consistent professional standards, and had tried to foster in every student the best possible work of which she was capable. In one case I was totally exonerated, but my relation to the other complainant was deemed to be in violation of the university's policy on "consensual amorous relations."

Consensual amorous relations are included in my university's sexual harassment policy. Thus, although I had sexually harassed no one, I was nominally in violation of sexual harassment policy. The "consensual amorous relation" in question was neither a sexual relation nor even a romantic, dating one; it was a teaching relation where both parties were interested in writing and talking about the erotic dynamics underpinning the student-teacher relation. Add to that adventuresome topic a teacher and a student whose styles tend toward the pedagogy of shocking performance—and what was never anything but a teaching relation found itself proscribed by university policy.

To explain what happened, it must be said that this teaching relation broke down, not because of its adventurous style but in the way so many teaching relations fall apart: more than once I told the student her work was not satisfactory; she did not accept my judgments and became increasingly suspicious and angry. Of course, there will always be students angry at professors, students who refuse to accept negative evaluations of their work; there will always be teaching relations which fail dramatically. No policy can protect our profession from the real and constant risk of failure to teach individual students. Both of the complaints against me stemmed from such failures. While personally, as a teacher, I cannot help but regret these impasses, wondering if and how I could have done better, what is relevant for this essay is not why the students filed complaints, but why it was possible to plausibly construe my professional behavior within the ambit of sexual harassment.

The complaints alleged sexual harassment proper, accusing me of behavior of which I was innocent: that I had attempted to get the students to have sex with me and that I had, when my advances were rejected, retaliated with negative evaluations of work or refusals to write letters of recommendation. The investigation found no evidence either of the "advances" or of the "retaliations"—in fact, it found these allegations to be implausible. Yet the Office of Affirmative Action—having accurately perceived my actual relations with students, having determined to their satisfaction that I was not guilty of the conduct alleged in the complaints—saw fit to chastise me for something of which there had been no complaint: a too intense, too personal, too volatile pedagogical relation with one student. This finding suggests an atmosphere in which sexual policy is so widely construed as not only to punish and restrict harassment but also to chill other relations, productive relations where it is not so easy to separate the erotic from the intellectual or the professional.

Antiharassment activists have come increasingly to see the difficulty in drawing a line between the sexual and the personal or social. Zealous to exclude the sexual from the pedagogical, many believe teacher-student relations should be neither social nor personal. Although I can see that a "strictly business" approach is probably the best way to guard against the sexual, I envision an enormous pedagogical loss from prohibiting interaction with the student as a person.

It is not only that such a sterilization of pedagogy goes against my own methods and talents. The irony is that this depersonalizing runs directly counter to the trend in feminist pedagogy. Even a cursory glance at feminist writing on teaching will yield a widespread affirmation of "the personal," as content and technique. The editors of the best-known collection of essays on feminist teaching tell us that a theme that recurs throughout the collection is, as they put it, "the transforming power of the personal as the subject and method of feminist education."[1] While feminists concerned with teaching affirm "the personal" as a way to foster women's learning, feminists working against sexual harassment target "personal" speech or behavior by the instructor as creating an environment hostile to women's education.

Personalizing pedagogy helps women become knowers; personalizing pedagogy obstructs women from getting an education. Stated like this, one can see the contradiction. Both of these propositions have in fact been upheld by feminist academics—sometimes by the very same people. The incongruity, however, has been obscured by the assumption that sexual harassers and feminist teachers were mutually exclusive categories. Personal pedagogy by feminists fosters women's learning, but when sexist pigs get personal they curtail women's opportunities for education. My own incongruous situation as a feminist accused of sexual harassment made this contradiction visible. The unprofessional, personal behavior that ran afoul of sexual harassment policy was in fact my application of feminist pedagogical methods; as a feminist, I had assumed that the side of the equation that held the personal to be good applied to me. But because harassment policy is written for sex-blind universal application, the category proscribed by the university as unprofessional can, ironically, encompass feminist pedagogy itself.

Breaking down the barrier between the professional and the personal has been central in the feminist effort to expand the institution of knowledge to include what and how women know. Since the beginning of the movement for women's studies, feminist academics have criticized the way a certain professionalization of knowledge denied connections between knowledge and the world, a process which rendered many of women's protofeminist responses illegitimate. Because authorized knowledge tended to exclude what women knew, feminist scholars were skeptical of lines demarcating the professional from the unprofessional. Feminist teachers saw the inclusion of the personal within the academic as a way to consider thoughts, responses, and insights which would not traditionally be recognized as knowledge.

In fact, sexual harassment is itself an excellent example of something which had traditionally been dismissed as personal and subjective but which feminists heard as something women knew. Sexual harassment would never have been recognized and conceptualized had feminists not been devoted to learning from women's personal perspectives. Catharine MacKinnon's *Sexual Harassment of Working Women*, which defined the terms for the feminist legal campaign against harassment, not only demonstrates thorough professional and theoretical knowledge of the law but also makes clear how it is dependent on legitimating the personal as knowledge. In her preface, MacKinnon writes:

I hope to bring to the law something of the reality of women's lives. The method and evidence chosen for this task deserve comment. To date, there are no "systematic" studies of sexual harassment in the social-scientific sense. So how do I know it exists? . . . Women's consciousness erupts through fissures in the socially knowable. *Personal* statements direct from daily life, in which we say more than we know, may be the primary form in which such experiences exist in social space; at this point they may be their only accessible form.[2]

When we speak personally, "we say more than we know": that is, we produce knowledge even the woman speaking cannot recognize as knowledge. What women know ("women's consciousness") has been excluded from recognizable, sanctioned knowledge ("the socially knowable") and thus relegated to "the personal." In keeping with feminist epistemology, MacKinnon insists that, to include women's knowledge in the professional sphere (here "the law"), she must cross the line that separates the professional from the personal.

As MacKinnon and many other feminists made clear, sexual harassment was rendered invisible precisely by its relegation to the realm of the personal. Complaints to authorities and attempts at legal redress were dismissed as the woman's personal problem or the man's personal failing. As merely a personal matter, it was thus not considered discrimination—which is social and political and which, to be legally actionable, must involve a professional realm such as employment or education. Had feminists not challenged the boundary that separates the personal from the professional, sexual harassment could never have been recognized and made illegal.

It is thus particularly ironic that, as a solution to the problem of sexual harassment, feminists are proposing we police the line separating the professional from the personal in the institution of knowledge. While for more than two decades feminists in the academy have been struggling to cross that line as a way of getting access to women's knowledge and as a way of promoting women's learning, today there are feminists who advocate closing the border between the professional and the personal.

In our culture it is women who are more likely to blur the boundaries between the professional and the personal. Whether we think this blurring inevitable or contingent, good or bad, as long as it is something women are more apt than men to do, as feminists we should be particularly careful to avoid instituting professional standards that women are more likely than men to fail to meet.

It would not be the first time that rules intended to protect women should end up working to women's professional disadvantage. Anyone familiar with feminist history immediately thinks of the laws setting maximum working hours or maximum lifting weights for women—which, although presumably intended to protect from physical harm, had the effect of excluding women from a large number of gainful occupations. And, more often than not, such protective restrictions have involved sexual matters.

It is worth remembering that the most consistent reason given for not allowing women into men's professional spaces has been that women will by their very presence sexualize the space and disrupt business (think of the recently questioned ban on women on battleships). I think that as long as our society can conflate women with sex and make women bear a disproportionate share of the burden of human sexuality, we need to be aware of how measures supposedly against sex consistently end up working against women. That would be the final turn of the sexual harassment screw, though not at all unprecedented in the history of the suppression of women.

In *Sexual Harassment of Working Women,* MacKinnon warns us against precisely such dangers, which would follow from misconstruing sexual harassment as a traditional morality issue: "When it becomes clear that such protections of delicacy and purity have worked women's exclusion from the decisive arenas of social life . . . more moralism looks like more of the problem" (172–73). She puts it in a kind of feminist shorthand: "The aura of the pedestal [is] more rightly understood as the foundation of the cage" (172). Wanting to avoid repeating the gesture which throughout history, in the guise of protecting women, has restricted women's opportunities, MacKinnon argues forcefully for considering sexual harassment, as her subtitle puts it, "a case of sex discrimination": in order better to protect women from professional and educational deprivation, sexual harassment must be legally prosecuted not because it is sexual but because it is sexist.

MacKinnon and other feminist scholars and lawyers were successful in getting sexual harassment legally defined as sex discrimination under Title VII (covering employment) and, presumably, under Title IX (covering education). Yet, in the decade and a half since that clear feminist victory, the feminist definition of sexual harassment appears to be fading, giving way to a more traditional understanding in which this behavior is condemnable because it is sexual. In the last few years, sexual harassment has become a high-profile national issue: Anita Hill and Robert Packwood can serve as markers of the issue's move to the center of national attention. Since explicit sexual content is likely to sensationalize any story, now that sexual harassment is widely recognized, it is widely misrecognized as a form of perverted sexuality rather than a garden-variety type of sexism.

Whereas there is a long tradition both in the culture at large and within the academy of condemning and punishing sexuality, our society and campuses have only recently begun to censure and prosecute sexism. Given the striking novelty of measures against sexism, it is no wonder that they might tend to revert back to the old, familiar idea that society must regulate that dangerous thing, sexuality—for the purpose of protecting women, of course. The fact that sexual harassment is offensive to women is understood through the traditional paradigm which sees sexuality as an affront to women. This would be but one more example of a recurrent tendency in the history of ideas: a new idea, in the course of its diffusion, becomes assimilated to an older idea.

There are signs that harassment is being taken out of the context of the larger struggle against sex discrimination. At my university, there are posters everywhere saying sexual harassment will not be tolerated, and several times in the last few years brochures have been distributed to the faculty outlining our sexual harassment policy; all administrators and many departments have gone through sexual harassment workshops. Seeking to go beyond reactive, punitive measures, the university is thus finally attempting to educate its community about sexual harassment. Yet this high-profile attention to harassment contrasts with the near total absence of like attention to other forms of sex discrimination (or, for that matter, other kinds of discrimination). If harassment is a form of sex discrimination, it should be fought within a broad-based campaign whose central target is discrimination. If harassment is despicable and illegal because it deprives women of the opportunity to get an education, other forms of discrimination that likewise deprive women are equally pernicious. Singled out as if it were a special sort of danger, harassment is more likely to be interpreted as bad not because it is sexist but because it is sexual.

All but forgotten are common nonsexual forms of sexual harassment—like the engineering professor who regularly tells his classes that women can't be engineers, working toward that self-fulfilling prophecy by encouraging his male students while making sure his female students feel stupid whenever they ask a question or don't understand. This behavior fits the legal definition of sexual harassment: it is the creation of a hostile environment by harassing behavior which discriminates on the basis of sex. When we remember to target sexist but nonsexual behavior within our campaign against harassment, we resist the sensationalism that wants to focus on the sexual and we recall that the real affront to women is sexism, the real threat to women is our relegation to second-class status and our exclusion from opportunities.

The fundamental question should not be whether students are treated sexually but whether, as Adrienne Rich puts it, women students are taken seriously.[3] The world-renowned philosophy professor who thinks women can't be philosophers—who demeans women in his class and refuses to take their work seriously, mentoring his bright male students while making his equally bright female students doubt their abilities—is doing profound damage to his women students. The fact that he has no sexual interest in them does not lessen the damage he does. His sexist but nonsexual behavior should be treated the same as that of his colleague in geology who gets female students alone under pretext of interest in their work and touches them inappropriately, exposing the fact that he was interested not in their work but their bodies. Both of these men deprive women of the environment necessary to foster their learning. That, and not the one man's lechery, is the crime.

Just as not all sexism is sexual, not all sexuality is sexist. When we understand harassment as bad because sexual, not only do we narrow our focus and leave undisturbed all the creeps who have been systematically discouraging women students in nonsexual ways, we also risk too broad a focus which would target the sexual per se and censure appearances of the sexual which benefit the causes of women and education. While all the hard scientists who wouldn't think of taking on a woman as a research assistant or postdoc proceed unaffected by the campaign against sexual harassment, gay and lesbian teachers who include discussion of homosexuality in "straight" courses might be accused by their homophobic students of creating a hostile environment through "unnecessary" discussion of sexuality, or feminists who expose the misogyny of pornography might be accused by offended male students of sexual harassment.

The intersection of sexuality and sexism has been a key site for feminist inquiry. Feminists widely agree that, in a society like ours, sexuality is a primary arena of sexism. Women's sexuality has been variously exploited, assaulted, deformed, condemned, and denied—each tactic representing another aspect of misogynist culture. But feminists have differed in our responses to the pervasiveness of a sexuality in which men are desiring subjects and women dehumanized objects. While some feminists see sexuality as the means of dehumanizing women, others of us believe we must claim our sexuality in order to be fully human. While one group of feminists has sought ways of restricting male sexuality, feminists of another stripe have worked to explore alternatives to the dominant form of sexuality.

In the early 1980s this split within feminism burst into an angry battle when a group of feminists organized an extremely effective legal campaign against pornography. In response to this campaign, another group of feminists questioned whether pornography deserved this singular focus and worried that singling out such an explicitly sexual form of sexism would play into the hands of the reactionary and decidedly antifeminist movement for traditional morality. Many of this second group of feminists publicly declared their enjoyment of pornography as part of women's claim to be desiring subjects.

This debate on pornography was belligerent but very useful: it made it clear that there was more than one feminist view of sex. Although I definitely side with those who feel it essential that women explore sexuality, I can see that it is the two sides together that best represents a feminist view of sex: sex is, at one and the same time, both central to the oppression of women and central to our liberation. Feminists in the academy have benefited from this debate; it has contributed substantially to our understanding of the complex interaction between sexuality and sexism. But outside the realms of feminist theory, not only have few people heard of this debate, but most assume that the antipornography position is *the* feminist position, that all feminists share this view of sex.

Harassment policy hails from the wing of feminism that produced the antipornography movement. (For example, Catharine MacKinnon has been a key legal theorist for both campaigns.) Unlike pornography, however, sexual harassment has produced no real debate within feminism. Whereas there were feminists willing to come out pro-pornography, no feminist would want to be for sexual harassment. To be sure, I am not going to suggest that feminists defend sexual harassment. My point, rather, is that the same radically negative view of sex explicitly challenged in relation to pornography has proceeded—unchallenged by any pro-sex feminist voice—to determine university policy. I want here precisely to question not the effort to curtail sexual harassment but the assumption currently skewing the antiharassment campaign that sexuality per se is harmful to women.

One of the symptoms of this antisex position is the inclusion of prohibitions against "consensual" relations in harassment policies. If harassment is, precisely, "unwanted" sexual advances, it would have to be defined as the opposite of "wanted" sexual advances. To include consensual relations within harassment policy suggests that sexual advances are never wanted, that the sexual is always offensive—if not to the individual woman or student then certainly to the institution. I know of a professor suspended without pay for a year for violating his university's policy on consensual relations although his student paramour had not filed a complaint; in fact, she asserted that it was the best relationship she'd ever had.

The reasoning behind the prohibition of consensual relations holds that, because of the power differential, students are not in a position freely to consent. This idea is solidly rooted in feminist theory: it is based upon an analysis of the institution of heterosexuality in a society where women are economically disadvantaged. Most women in such a society must depend upon sexual relations with men (ranging from legal marriage to literal prostitution) for economic survival. In a footnote to *Sexual Harassment of Working Women*, MacKinnon questions "whether, under conditions of male supremacy, the notion of consent has any real meaning for women . . . . whether it is a structural fiction to legitimize the real coercion built into the normal social definitions of heterosexual intercourse. . . . [whether] consent is not normally given but taken" (298n. 8). Students cannot "really" consent to sex with professors for the same reasons (power differential, economic/professional dependency) that women cannot "really" consent to sex with men.

While I fully accept the validity of this analysis (what Adrienne Rich has called "compulsory heterosexuality"),[4] I do not think the solution is to deny people with less power the right to consent. This is, I believe, the standard, protectionist path, which protects women by restricting us. As a feminist, I recognize that women are at a disadvantage but believe that denying women the right to consent further infantilizes us, denies us our full humanity. Prohibition of consensual relations is based in the assumption that when a woman says yes she really means no. I cannot help but think that this proceeds from the same logic in which when a woman says no she really means yes. The first assumption is protectionist; the second reflects the logic of harassment. Common to both is the assumption that women do not know what we want, that someone else, in a position of greater knowledge and power, knows better.

Around 1990 I became aware that universities were including prohibitions against consensual relations in their harassment policies. As a feminist theorist, I was troubled by the unstated assumption that women were frail victims, threatened by the sexual. As a pro-sex feminist, I was disturbed that an antisex position was being taken as *the* feminist position, unchallenged by any other feminist voice. As a woman who, when a student, had aggressively pursued sexual relations with teachers, I felt my desire erased and the way it had made me feel powerful denied. I began talking to my friends around the country, feminist academics of my generation, and discovered that a large number of us had had sexual relations with teachers either as undergraduates or graduate students. These relations had been part of our embrace of the intellectual life. Yet, in the wake of a new feminist line on teacher-student sex, these common experiences were buried in silence. No one from this huge cohort was talking about her prior consensual relations with teachers. No feminist who had pursued such relations questioned the revisionism which redefined those relations as harassment.

While I recognized the recently understood dangers of such liaisons, I was nonetheless concerned that an entire stretch of experience was being denied, consigned to silence. As an academic and a feminist, I wanted to see discussion, instead of the silent installation of one reigning interpretation in the place of another. I proposed to organize a conference on teacher-student sex at my university with speakers representing a broad range of perspectives: from consensual sex as a covert form of harassment to a historical perspective going back to Plato, Rousseau, and Heloise and Abelard. If we were living through a radical change in the understanding of the teacher-student relation, I thought it our duty as intellectuals and teachers to study and discuss that change.

To my great surprise, a number of feminist faculty protested this conference proposal. They felt that any critical discussion of harassment policy would aid and abet harassers. I felt I was being told that there could be no public feminist disagreement on this issue. I did not wish to be in a hostile relation with feminist colleagues at the university where I had just begun working. Given the intensity of the resistance and the volatility of the issue, we decided to give up the conference (still in its early planning stages) and replace it with a conference on the more general topic of the personal in pedagogy.

Some who had protested the original conference considered "the personal" just a euphemism for "the sexual." I was taken aback by this response, given the history of "the personal" as a valued term within feminist pedagogy. I did not, at the time, understand that I had entered into the heart of a contradiction in the nexus of feminism and sexual harassment. When certain feminists celebrate the personal as the royal road to women's consciousness, they assume that "the personal" does not include the sexual. This is possible, I guess, because of the traditional understanding of women as not sexual. As soon as "the personal" involves people presumed to be sexual—like men or women who have proposed a conference on sex—"the personal" becomes a suspicious, dangerous category, and some feminists begin to demand silence and strictly professional behavior.

It was a year after this uproar over my conference proposal that the complaints against me were filed and another year before the determination was issued. By the time the determination came down, it had been three years since I had begun publicly questioning the policy prohibiting consensual relations. The specific finding in my case thus presented the most perfect irony: I was found in violation of the very policy that I had set about to protest.

I thought the prohibition of consensual relations was an incongruity in a policy against unwanted sexual advances. The Office of Affirmative Action didn't see a contradiction in the policy but instead found me to be in contradiction with—that is, in violation of—the harassment policy. I had felt free to publicly question the consensual sex policy precisely because—as a recognized feminist theorist who was not having sex with students—I assumed my position would be taken as a disagreement over feminist strategy rather than as an expression of self-interest. I did not realize it was possible to apply the policy to the sort of relations I *was* having with students.

Following feminist pedagogical tradition, I had engaged in personal relations with students—that is to say I had related to them not just as interchangeable receptacles into which I poured knowledge, but as people. As a pro-sex feminist, I had assumed that involved recognizing—and, when pedagogically useful, commenting upon—the sexual as part of the relation between people. By sexual here, I do not of course mean sex acts but rather the erotic dynamics which intertwine with other aspects of human interaction. It is precisely because I believe it not possible to neatly separate the sexual from other sorts of relations that I find the movement to bar the sexual from pedagogy not only dangerous but supremely impractical.

I would rather find some way to apply the criterion proposed by Rich—taking women students seriously. While sexualization is no doubt frequently a sign that the other person is not being taken seriously (as in "he just wants her for her body"), most of us would recognize that in our own sexual relationships (or those we would like to have) our partner is one of the people, if not the person, we take most seriously. While desire can indeed be demeaning and dehumanizing, it can also be the mark of profound esteem. The determining factor would seem to be whether the one who desires takes the desired other seriously as a person, as a subject with a will of her own, whether desire can recognize in its object another desiring subject.

That is why the question of whether sexual advances are wanted is absolutely crucial. Unwanted sexual advances, in particular advances which persist despite the other having made clear her lack of interest, definitely signal a sexuality which does not take the other seriously. This sort of imposition is properly called harassment.

The urgency of harassment as a threat to the education of women has been taken as a reason for a unified feminist front that cannot tolerate disagreement within the ranks. However, the very centrality of harassment to the nexus of sex and sexism demands we carefully consider how the issue is framed, and feminists think best when we openly explore our differences. There has not yet been a feminist debate on sexual harassment. Before harassment is defined solely by traditional sexual morality, feminists who fight for women's sexuality must join the discussion.

Four Resisting Reasonableness

In *Feminist Accused of Sexual Harassment*, in the chapter called "Consensual Amorous Relations," I argued that, whatever the actual policy on consensual relations, the very inclusion of such relations within harassment policies is a theoretical mistake with far-reaching practical consequences.[1] As I wrote in the book:

> *Their very inclusion within harassment policies* indicates that consensual relations are themselves considered a type of sexual harassment. Sexual harassment has always been defined as *unwanted* sexual attention. But with this expansion into the realm of consensual relations, the concept can now encompass sexual attention that is reciprocated and very much welcome. This reconfigures the notion of harassment, suggesting that what is undesirable finally is not unwelcome attention but sexuality per se. Rather than some sexuality being harassing because of its unwanted nature, the inference is that sexuality is in and of itself harassment. (32)

I would still insist on the danger of this inclusion, a danger we all ought to be able to agree upon, however we feel about teacher-student sex. I hope that even those who are completely opposed to any sex between teachers and students will accept the idea that consensual sex must not be treated as harassment. If we want people to take sexual harassment seriously, it is imperative to distinguish it from any form of consenting relations, even or especially those forms some people might find objectionable.

Campuses continue to treat consensual relations *within* their harassment policies, which suggests I must continue to make my argument. But since I've already made that argument in the book, I would like here to explore another aspect of consensual relations policies, one that seems more controversial (given the response to my book, I should perhaps say even more controversial) and which I'm still trying to work out.

Every single reporter who interviewed me about the book responded to my careful explanation of the danger of treating consensual relations as harassment by glibly agreeing and then quickly moving on to ask, "but what about" treating consensual relations as a "conflict of interest." And in every single interview, I felt I did not answer that question well. I'm hoping finally to give this question the thoughtful response it deserves.

■　　■　　■

Let's start with a couple I know: two women madly in love with each other for about a year now—one in her early forties, the other in her mid-thirties, both out lesbians through their adult lives. This feels to them like real love, the kind that lasts, and both have been around enough to make that sort of judgment. When one woman speaks of the other, her eyes glisten, her face radiates. In conversation she is often voicing anger at various injustices, but when the subject of their relationship comes up, the muscles in her neck and face relax, her breathing slows—witnessing this feels like a glimpse of love.

Now, given my topic, I'm sure you've already guessed what I'm about to tell you. Not only are these women lovers, they are also teacher and student. Both are in the anthropology department of a state university in the Pacific Northwest. The younger is a doctoral student writing her dissertation; the older a tenured professor supervising that dissertation. After they were already working together, they found themselves in love. They chose both to act upon their feelings for each other and to maintain their productive working relation. They thus are proceeding in complete and utter violation of their university's policy on consensual relations. Their love must remain a secret. If they were discovered, it could destroy both of their careers. Yet they're planning to spend their lives together.

This couple has the good luck to work in a department that is unusually lesbian-friendly. Both have long lived comfortably in lesbian subculture. Yet they find themselves now in a dark and scary closet. As I've emphasized, perhaps to the point of some sappiness, these two women find themselves not just in heat but in love. In the sort of love that makes them constitute themselves as a couple. Now, while some of us have reservations about coupledom, it is worth noting that, in the context of today's academic policies, it is the romantic couple who run the greatest risk.

Consensual relations policies actually pose little threat to all the teachers and students who continue to have the occasional fling, the moment of passion, the friendly shtup. Not only is it much easier to hide a casual or short-term sexual connection, it might even be sexier to hide it. But something in the nature of the romantic couple longs for public recognition. Marriage, of course, immediately comes to mind. While we may indeed be suspicious of that peculiar institution, we probably want at least the possibility of having our love recognized. We might not want marriage, but we don't want the closet either.

While I find this antiromantic twist in contemporary academic policy quite interesting, it is not really what I need my couple to exemplify. They're here because I need their romance to disrupt the consensus of reasonableness which currently dominates the conversation on teacher-student sex.

Whereas teacher-student sex has certainly been portrayed in the lurid tones of incest and pedophilia, suggesting it to be an abomination against nature for any teacher and any student to lie together or even play together, nowadays the official discussion is more likely to be in the moderate and legalistic tones of "conflict of interest." While it seems relatively easy to demonstrate the dangers of erotophobic moralizing, it is not so easy to voice objection to policies that appear designed not to prohibit sexuality but simply to avoid "conflict of interest." While it may be heroic to appear pro-sex and anti-moralism, it's not so cool to seem irresponsible and unreasonable.

In 1990, the university where I teach had a policy stating that "consenting amorous or sexual relationships between instructor and student are unacceptable." That was it, simply "unacceptable," a blanket prohibition on sex between two categories of people, an absolute generality which could even mean that, since teaching assistants find themselves in the indelicate situation of being at once instructors and students, the policy would forbid them from masturbating.

Sometime around 1993 our university became aware of the immoderate nature of this policy and adopted a new, thoroughly reasonable policy. The new policy recognizes that students and teachers will enter into amorous relations and tells us what to do when that happens. The faculty member should notify her dean in writing of the relationship and arrange to avoid conflict of interest by immediately giving up any supervisory or evaluative relation to the student. If the student is in the teacher's class, arrangements should be made for someone else to grade the student; if the professor is on a graduate student's committee, she should immediately be replaced by another faculty member.

The new policy represents a clear advance over the old one—from just about any point of view. It is more practical, more realistic, more liberal, easier to live with, easier to enforce—not to mention less vulnerable to jokes and ridicule than the primitive version. It sounds more like a policy, less like a taboo. As we moved from the early to the mid-nineties, the nationwide trend was toward this sort of reasoning. More and more campuses adopted such moderate policies, and everyone seemed to agree that the issue was not really sex but rather conflict of interest. I felt disarmed by the new policies. They did not say sex was bad, only that if you had to have sex, you needed to stop being teacher and student. It was all so reasonable, who could resist?

Well, that lesbian couple I was just telling you about, for one.

They work at a university with a similar policy. When they realized they were in love, all they had to do was stop working together: the student find another dissertation director, the professor resign from the student's committee. Had they done that, their love would have been legit, their careers safe. But instead they chose to violate the policy and risk their careers. In the realm of the old moralistic taboo, the question would have been, how could they sleep together? But in our new, apparently less moralistic terms, the scandalous question is, how could they refuse to do the reasonable thing?

It is precisely this refusal to comply that put them in this essay. Their disobedience suggests that they might help us see beyond the new policies' seeming universal reasonableness.

Let's look at this situation from the student's point of view. This student is in her mid-thirties; she entered the doctoral program after having worked for more than a decade as a well-paid, respected professional. Her research interests had grown out of her professional experience. When she began her doctoral studies, she was dismayed to find herself "treated like a student," by which she means treated like someone who has no knowledge, whose professional experience does not count, treated like a receptacle for the professors' knowledge. In short, she felt treated like a child.

In contrast with the general attitude in her department, there was one professor who treated her like an adult, respected her professional experience, the knowledge she brought with her, her ideas. This respect did not preclude criticism. On the contrary, this professor was more critical of her writing, setting higher standards, and demanding more than did the other faculty. The criticism was intrinsic to the respect; it meant she didn't feel she was being babied, patronized, spoken down to. She chose to work with the one professor who regarded her as an adult. This teacher didn't impose her own ideas on the student but rather fostered the development of the student's thinking. The student felt this was the sort of relation in which she could work best, in which she would do her best work.

Our student here is, admittedly, a particular sort of student, a strong-willed, highly motivated older student who comes into graduate school with a clear sense of purpose. She needed a particular sort of mentoring relation, one that would not insult her sense of her own considerable experience. She found that in only one teacher in her department; she knew she would not be able to replace it. For this student, the reasonable policy demanded an unreasonable sacrifice. In order to be in compliance, she was supposed to find a new professor to work with. To change dissertation directors was, however, no small thing: it meant putting her work at risk.

This unusually self-possessed doctoral student found one professor who respected her as an adult, who recognized her as a person. And that teacher who recognized her, who saw her worth and her merit and her power, desired her and came to love her. The one professor who saw her as a person rather than a student came to want more of a relation to that person than one defined by the roles of teacher and student. I want to suggest that the very recognition and respect which made this such a productive professional relation are inseparable from the possibility of falling in love.

The policy asks the student to make what it assumes is a reasonable choice: would you rather love this woman or work with her? The policy demands that she sort out her feelings and decide whether those feelings are sexual or intellectual, professional or romantic. Do I love her for how she teaches me, or do I love her so much that I want to replace her with another teacher? The policy does not recognize that we might not want to have a reasonable, moderate relation either to our love or to our work.

This couple takes us outside the logic of the policy. Whereas the policy represents the norm, these women inhabit the extreme of both the amorous and the pedagogical relation: in each other they feel they've found their one true love; they have an intense one-on-one working relation which likewise denies the possibility of substitution. This sense of "the only one" bespeaks passion and represents a logic alien to the world of reasonable calculation. In the world of their relation, the reasonableness of choice and substitution can only represent loss, tragedy, betrayal, and incomprehension.

I take this couple as exemplary not because they are the norm but because they represent an extreme we disregard at great risk. Where the policy would regulate us based upon a norm, I would resist this regulation in the name of a relation far better than the norm. I see in this extreme a sort of ideal, an old-fashioned romantic ideal, that work and life, mind and body, thought and passion can come together across the divide which too often separates them. Such separations are regrettably all too normal in academic life. Do we want an ethics based upon that sad norm? Do we want policies to enforce that norm? To punish those queer enough to pursue the ideal?

I'd like to look at consensual relations policy from the standpoint of this extreme relation. I initially signaled the couple's exorbitance by introducing them as "madly in love." While I want to hold on to the romantic force of their excessiveness, I would now like to situate it within their *academic* relation. I want to suggest that, from the point of view of the pedagogical norm, the dissertator-supervisor relation is already in itself an exorbitant relation.

First of all, a dissertator is, by definition, at the very edge of student identity. Literally at the end of her studies, the dissertator is no longer simply a student, already within the rite of passage to professor. Dissertator is a liminal identity: a dissertator is a student who cannot be comfortable with being a student. Although our exemplary dissertator returned to graduate school with more independence than the norm, impatience with being treated "like a student" is no doubt endemic to dissertator status.

The student who is no longer quite a student works within an unusual pedagogical relation. Whereas the most common pedagogical relation lasts for a few months, with teacher and student meeting only in the company of dozens of other students, this is a long-term, one-on-one relation. Dissertator and supervisor commonly work together for several years and normally meet tête-à-tête. If we take as the norm the relation between a student and the instructor whose course she takes for one term, the relation between dissertator and supervisor is exorbitant.

In the realm of pedagogy, the dissertator-supervisor couple represents an extreme like the romantic couple in the realm of amorous relations. My point in drawing this analogy is not to suggest that dissertator-supervisor pairs are latent romantic couples. The romantic couple is here rather to put us in the mood to prize excessiveness. The moderate policies with their reasonable concern about conflict of interest are in fact based upon a conception of teaching as an uncaring, impersonal relation, a relation where simple calculations of interest are possible, teaching reduced to its lowest common denominator.

Earlier I noted that current academic relations policies are in fact more hospitable to casual sex than to serious romance. I see this now not as an anomaly but as entirely consistent with the norm of casual, short-term relations upon which the policies are based. In the view of these policies, it is normal human behavior to contract relations—whether amorous *or* pedagogical—which involve minimal entanglement, relations in which it is easy to maintain separation between the parties, relations which don't involve excessive investment or confusion of interest, relations easy to dissolve should things become complicated.

Upon reading an early draft of this essay, one of my dissertators, who is rather militantly antimonogamous, was bothered by its celebration of the romantic couple, its privileging the couple over casual sex. Her query is well-taken, and I'd like to respond to it. My argument is with the casual, no-entanglement norms of academic policy. In *this* context, in the context of this argument, in the context of academic policy, I feel romantic love can provide a discourse with the power to counter the businesslike, legalistic reasonableness which would regulate our pedagogical relations. While in the amorous realm the long-term, one-on-one relationship is certainly normative, in the pedagogical realm it is practically queer.

My celebration of romance here is not about sex; it's about teaching. My exemplary couple resisted the consensus of reasonableness not by having sex but by refusing to give up their pedagogical relation. I too want to resist contemporary policy by prizing pedagogical relations. Whereas the policies take as their model the standard casual short-term pedagogical encounter, I prefer the dissertator-supervisor relation because it deviates from the norm in an ideal way, a way that allows us to think about pedagogy not as it all too often is, but as it sometimes can be, fortunately.

I hope my dissertator will understand what I'm saying here not through her sexual politics but through her pedagogical experience, that she will understand what I'm saying through the complicated, intense, and productive relation we share. She and I are not in love, we're not having sex (at least not with each other), but we have been working together for five years, since she entered our doctoral program. She took her first class from me in the fall of 1993 and two more graduate seminars in the next year. Four years ago I chaired her academic review; two and a half years ago, her preliminary examinations. Since then we've been working together on her dissertation. In those years, we've met countless times one-on-one to talk about her writing, and more recently to prepare her for the job market.

It is of course my role to evaluate her. When she took my classes, I graded her papers and oral presentations and gave her semester grades. On her examinations, I had to say whether or not I thought she should pass. And in a few months I will chair her dissertation defense and pronounce whether or not I think she has earned a Ph.D. In my evaluations, I embody some version of professional standards, judging whether or not she has met those standards. Teaching her is not, however, merely evaluation. By advising her on how to revise her writing, how to prepare for her examinations, I help her meet my standards, get her ready to pass my evaluations. The supervisor is not only judge but also coach.

When academic relations policies worry about "conflict of interest," they are thinking about the professor's evaluation of the student. If the professor cares too much about the student, loves or desires the student, or feels hurt and rejected by the student, then it will affect the evaluation, taint the evaluation with subjectivity. But can a professor objectively evaluate the work of someone whom she has been coaching for years? I would argue that the supervisor is, by the very nature of her role, inevitably too close, too invested, and definitely cares too much. I want my dissertator to succeed—

because she is "*my* student," because her success reflects on me, her achievements afford me prestige. My considerable investment of time and energy in her progress as well as my narcissistic investment in my own excellence as a teacher make me an interested party in the dissertator's success.

The policy assumes that if we can separate pedagogy from amorous relations, we can avoid conflict of interest. But thinking about the relation between dissertator and supervisor suggests that *no policy* can shield us from the potential for conflict of interest, that in fact conflict of interest goes with the territory.

Supervising a dissertator involves not only evaluation and advising; it also includes actual advocacy, an aspect most prominent during the student's jobseeking. When my dissertator went on the job market this fall, I advised her on her application letters, her vita, and other supporting material. But my most important task was to write a letter of recommendation for her dossier, to say what I could to persuade hiring committees of her excellence. This letter—a standard part of the dissertation supervisor's job description—is an act of advocacy whose conflicted relation to evaluation bears remarking.

Everyone complains that recommendations are inflated prose, impossible exercises in which the writer is forced both to exaggerate and to convey authenticity. I consider this stylistic problem symptomatic of a basic contradiction in the professor's position. We are supposed to write as if we were objective evaluators, judging the student by the application of professional standards, but we are in fact writing as devoted advocates trying to get our students jobs. We cannot admit that we are writing as advocates, a fact everyone nonetheless knows. The recommendation writer's relation to her student is a devotion that dare not speak its name.

We don't need to fall in love with our dissertators to find ourselves in a compromising situation. Our academic relation in itself is enough to produce conflict of interest. The conflict is not between pedagogy and love, but between two aspects of the pedagogical relation, evaluation and advocacy.

In mid-December I got a phone call from my dissertator, announcing she'd gotten an MLA interview. She called knowing her news would make me happy, and it did. I felt very much like I did when I myself got job interviews. A few days later I got a similar call from another of my grad students. Same tone of excitement in her voice, exact same opening statement: "I have good news." Except this student was not on the job market. Not quite a dissertator yet, this student is currently working with me to prepare for her preliminary examinations. She called to announce that all her English 101 students had passed. This was her first time teaching 101, a freshman composition course in which the instructor does not determine who passes and which a significant number of students fail.

Having one's students pass freshman comp at our university turns out to be not unlike having one's students get MLA interviews. In both cases the student succeeds in the eyes of outside evaluators, professional colleagues who don't know the student except on paper. In both cases, the actual teacher advises and roots for the student, but is outside the evaluation process.

The first-time 101 TA was overjoyed her students all passed, and she wanted to share her sense of accomplishment with me, her teacher. When she phoned, her students' achievement became my student's achievement too. This almost uncanny redoubling between her pride in her students and my pride in her suggests a connection between the two extremes of teaching in our department, between English 101 and English 990 (the number under which she is registered as my dissertator).

I've been talking about pedagogy in 990 for a while; I'd like now to tell you a bit about 101. In fact I've never taught 101, but I've learned a good deal about it from my dissertators, who all have. As they have explained to me, at our university freshman composition is organized to isolate evaluation from all other aspects of the student-teacher relation. At the end of the semester, the students' writing is evaluated by other 101 instructors. The actual teacher functions only as a coach, preparing them for evaluation by someone else. As a coach and then possibly as an advocate. For example, the TA who phoned to say all her students passed went on to correct herself—actually two hadn't passed but she had appealed and they had passed on appeal.

A teacher who cares about her students—who knows how hard they have worked, knows the sort of obstacles they have faced, in short, a teacher who sees students as people—may not be able to evaluate their work objectively. In freshman composition this problem is solved by divorcing the functions of evaluation and coaching.

I believe that the conflict addressed by the composition grading structure is a conflict endemic to pedagogy, the conflict between judging and caring. This is also the conflict of interest addressed by consensual relations policies, designed to keep instructors from evaluating students about whom the instructor cares too much to be objective. In fact, our composition administrators seem to have hit upon a solution to pedagogical conflict of interest that is essentially the *same* as our campus's consensual relations policy. In both cases, the structure is designed to guard against a teacher's grading a person she cares about. But the recognition that this can be a problem not only in cases of amorous relations but also in the normal course of teaching composition suggests it's a problem not likely to be solved by anything as simple as separating out those instructors romantically involved with their students. What consensual relations policy presumes to be a conflict *between* love and pedagogy is actually a conflict *within* pedagogy.

Earlier I insisted that I wanted to view pedagogy from the standpoint of the dissertator-supervisor relation. And, while this excursion into freshman comp may seem to have taken us from one extreme to the other of the university teaching spectrum, we have, in fact, never left the confines of the relation to my dissertators. As I specified when introducing 101 into the essay, everything I know about it, I know from them. A look at 101 provided me with something quite useful for this essay—a confirmation of the claim that conflict of interest is intrinsic to pedagogy—and I got that look at 101 in and through my relation to dissertators. It is this peculiar structure which I would propose as a model. I propose we look at university pedagogy in general through the lens of the quite particular dissertator-supervisor relation. Such a method is undoubtedly perverse. Perhaps even literally. Rather than reach a general understanding via the norm, I choose to theorize via a relatively rare and marginal case, but it is one that happens to be my own personal pedagogical preference.

Having with this essay finally found the time to think about the question, I'd like to rephrase a remark I once made in haste, in the heat of the moment, and to wide misunderstanding. Seven years ago, at another lesbian and gay academic colloquium, I stated that graduate students were my sexual preference. Today, after thinking it through, I would say rather that dissertators are my pedagogical preference.

With this essay, I'm trying to theorize pedagogy in a way that resists the norm and that bases itself in my own particular preference, a way of theorizing I might want to call queer—if that word didn't already have another meaning in the present context. Rather than queer theorizing, then, let me call it exorbitant, or maybe romantic.

I prefer teaching dissertators precisely because they are liminal students, students who do not comfortably fit the role, who are not simply students. For example, they are generally in the indelicate situation of being both students and teachers. This means teaching someone who also has some experience of the other side of the pedagogical relation. When I work with dissertators on the obstacles in their writing, they often come to understand what I'm saying when they realize its resemblance to things they tell their composition students. Of course this doesn't mean our roles are interchangeable, but it does mean our relation is not as unidimensional as it would be with someone who is more simply a student.

Not only do I often talk about teaching with my dissertators, comparing notes from our different but related practices, I also sometimes get help from them with my own writing. Such is the situation which led to my dissertator complaining that in this essay I privilege the romantic couple. The fact that a dissertator is someone who can help me with my writing by judging it (in this case, negatively) suggests the greater range and flexibility of this relation, one in which I am not always teaching and she not always learning.

I prefer teaching someone who is *not just* a student to me. I prefer a wider, more diverse, more human relation. While that is my preference, I am not trying to claim it as the pedagogical norm. Most of my teaching is not so fulfilling, so intense, so rounded. In fact most of my teaching unfortunately resembles the casual, short-term, impersonal, uncaring relation that is the norm.

I believe, however, that it would benefit us to take as our pedagogical model not the norm but the best. While impatience with student identity is, as I said, endemic to dissertators, it is not restricted to them. There are sometimes in our classes—not only grad but undergrad—students who don't want to be "treated like students," students who are older, or just bolder, who want to learn, but find the student role demeaning and constrictive. I think our pedagogical policies ought to honor those students.

This essay takes as its pedagogical model the couple I began with. It is, to be sure, an exorbitant model. Doubly exorbitant: as far from the norm of dissertator-supervisor relations as the standard dissertator-supervisor relation is from the campus pedagogical norm. This amorous couple is my model because they prize their pedagogical relation unreasonably, and at considerable risk. I'm hoping that by showing us the exorbitant value of their pedagogical relation, they will help us view pedagogy with a less cost-effective, more romantic gaze.

Part Two The Stories

■ ■ ■

"In the fall of 1974 . . ."—thus opens the first of the five essays in part 2, opening with the promise of a story. In what follows, that opening gesture is frequently repeated. More than a third of the paragraphs in the first essay begin with such temporal cues—"About six months later," "A decade ago," "Sometime in 1978," "Last March." The frequency of the gesture suggests an urgency not only to tell a story but to locate the story in time.

That double exigency is shared by all the essays in part 2. Two of the essays open with the same gesture: "Half a dozen years ago" and "Twenty-three years ago." This classic storytelling gambit situates audience and narrator within a shared present moment in the aftermath of the story to be told. Such a gesture not only alludes to oral storytelling but also proffers the story as having happened, makes a claim to telling not only story but history.

All the essays in part 2 mention a date in their first sentence. The final essay begins: "The paper you are about to read was presented on October 3, 1999." This last essay takes these time markers to a new extreme of precision. We move from the years, seasons, and months of the earlier essays to days, hours, and minutes—6:32 P.M., 7:10 P.M.,

7:18 P.M.—as if the project of anecdotal theory were trying ultimately to home in on and finally catch the moment.

The essays in this section appear in chronological order, according to the date of their original composition. The first is the earliest piece in the collection. Written in 1991, it was meant to be only a little occasional piece, a twenty-minute talk for the MLA convention, not part of any larger project. Retrospectively, it looks like a first attempt at anecdotal theory.

Alluding to Dickens's masterpiece of storytelling, the title—"A Tale of Two Jacques"—explicitly presents this essay as "a tale." In fact the essay tells two stories that happened to me: the first takes place in the mid-seventies while I was a graduate student; the second "story" is a dream I had in 1991. The relation between the two is psychoanalytic: the story from my professional and theoretical youth provides background material for interpreting the dream. Both are about my relation to a theoretical text, Jacques Derrida's 1974 reading of Jacques Lacan.

Derrida's theoretical encounter with Lacan is itself focused on a tale, Edgar Allan Poe's "The Purloined Letter." Lacan read Poe's short story as a theoretical text; Derrida argues with Lacan's theory via his own reading of the story. Lacan and Derrida share the presupposition that correct theory is to be found in the tale. Rereading Lacan's and Derrida's theoretical texts in 1991, I found myself producing not a theoretical reading but another story.

If we take "A Tale of Two Jacques" as the first piece of anecdotal theory, if we look at it to see our point of departure, two characteristics stand out. (1) We find ourselves at a juncture where theory is so tangled with story that, rather than attaining a theoretical perspective, I find myself able only to tell stories about theory. (2) This tale of theory proliferates indicators of time, as if this first turn to anecdotal theory had something to do with a compulsion to mark time.

"The timing seemed perfect," I wrote in "A Tale of Two Jacques." Today, ten years later, I hear in this phrase the essay's insistence on timing, its impulse to mark time. Back in 1991, the phrase meant that it seemed the perfect moment to reconsider Derrida and Lacan:

enough time had elapsed since I had been emotionally invested in Derrida and Lacan to make me think I had distance, theoretical perspective. Six months before I wrote the essay, I thought to myself "the timing seemed perfect"—and that very night I had a nightmare about Derrida and Lacan. My smug declaration of perfect timing rings darkly ironic when immediately thereupon I find myself plunged into anxiety.

The timing would have been perfect, if only I could have kept the past behind me. If the past had only been behind me, then I could have attained theoretical perspective, I could have proceeded from story to theory. "A Tale of Two Jacques," however, proceeds not from story to theory, but from theory to story, and—in the tradition both of psychoanalysis and of tales of terror—the past will not let me go.

A couple months after writing "A Tale," I set out for the first time intentionally to theorize from personal anecdote. The second essay in part 2, "Knot a Love Story," was my first conscious attempt at anecdotal theory. The idea was to tell a story and then proceed to theory. But that was not quite what happened. As I nervously re-mark in the essay's conclusion, "I found myself continually falling back into story, adding more stories in the latter part which is supposed to be theory." "Knot a Love Story" ends up telling not one but three stories, proceeding not from story to theory, but from present to past, moving further back in time. The first story, the only one I originally intended to tell, was from my recent past; the second story returns to my graduate student days; the third to my literal childhood.

The theoretical model in this essay, as in the previous one, is psychoanalytic. But unlike "A Tale," which tells stories about psychoanalytic theory, "Knot" applies psychoanalytic theory in order to make sense of its stories. In short, whereas "A Tale" anecdotalizes theory, "Knot" theorizes anecdotes. In the first essay, the project of anecdotal theory is unconscious and retrospective; in the second essay it is conscious and straightforward. *Anecdotal Theory* has this double origin—beginning in these two little essays, written just months apart, in the contrasts and similarities between them.

While both essays conjoin psychoanalytic theory with storytelling, they involve different story genres. Both entail narrative genres with longstanding connections to psychoanalysis: "A Tale" plunges me into the horror story; "Knot" tangles with the love story. Both essays also manifest a fraught relation to temporality. In the horror story, I am frightened by my inability to keep the present free from the past; in "Knot a Love Story," I struggle to keep the present from dissolving into an anticipation of what is to come.

In "Knot a Love Story" this temporal struggle is my struggle with narrative: "This is not a love story, rather a story of falling in love. Narrative convention leads us to take 'falling in love' as the opening scene of a drama which will unfold. . . . Here, however, it is not the opening scene but the whole story. Recounting it, I feel the pull toward conventional closure. . . . My urge—as reader, writer, or protagonist—to turn this into a love story is massive."

This 1992 essay means to recount a moment, a moment where something happened, where I began to feel something I had not felt before. The only story the essay intends to tell is the story of that moment. But in the essay I find myself struggling against a massive urge to lodge that moment in a standard progression. Whereas the moment is in fact an opening—the occurrence of something new, something surprising—a narrative drive wants to press forward from that "opening" to "closure." This narrative drive would make that moment the opening scene of a standard drama, moving toward dénouement. "Dénouement," from the French, means untying, from "noue," knot. "Knot a Love Story" tries to focus on, hold onto, the knot, rather than press forward to its untying.

The knot may be anecdote itself. An anecdote is the account of a single incident, a single moment. But as narrative, anecdote may also tend to elicit an urge to embed the incident in a larger story. Such an urge would lead us away from contact with the singular moment into all-too-familiar directions—conventional narrative arcs, standard plots. This contradiction between capturing the singular moment and a drive to insert the moment within a familiar plot may be not just a problem for this particular story but a tension intrinsic to the anecdote.

According to Fineman's "History of the Anecdote," the anecdote "introduces an opening into the teleological . . . narration of beginning, middle, and end." Fineman, however, goes on to say that this opening that the anecdote produces "is something that is characteristically . . . plugged up by a teleological narration" (72). Fineman theorizes anecdote in relation to teleological narration, to a story whose course is determined by its ending. I did not know Fineman's "History of the Anecdote" when I wrote "Knot a Love Story." Trying for the first time to theorize from an anecdote, I experienced a tension between what I called opening and what I called closure. Fineman's theorization of the anecdote likewise speaks of opening and closure.

The love story, I would note, is among the most teleological of narrations. What I grappled with in terms of "falling in love" and "the love story" is, I think, the same knot Fineman describes as the relation between anecdote and teleological narration. The anecdote produces an opening in teleological narration, but that opening is also "characteristically" stopped up by teleological narration. The narrative contradiction in "Knot a Love Story" is, it would seem, characteristic of anecdote.

The quotation from Fineman about the characteristic plugging of anecdote is excerpted from a long, complex sentence. In that sentence the relation between teleological narration and anecdote is actually even more tangled. And, as Fineman describes it, the tangle gets sexy: "The opening . . . that is effected by the anecdote, the hole and rim—using psychoanalytic language, the orifice—traced out by the anecdote . . . is characteristically . . . plugged up by a teleological narration that . . . is . . . inspired by the seductive opening of anecdotal form" (72). The anecdote introduces an opening in teleological narration, but that very opening inspires a teleological narration which comes to close it up. Fineman's account of this relation boggles normal temporal logic: which comes first, anecdote or teleological narration? The logic here is circular; or rather, it is a knot.

Trying to portray the knot, Fineman's language turns sexual: anecdotal opening is a seductive orifice which inspires teleological plugging. This sounds not unlike the teleological drive as I describe it in "Knot a Love Story": "Recounting it, I feel the pull toward conventional closure: did we do it?" Fineman's thread and mine cross at the juncture of anecdote and desire. "Knot" was my attempt to tell of the moment a desire arose. My project of recounting a moment was—though I did not call it such at the time—anecdotal. Wanting to tell an anecdote about the appearance of desire, I seem to have stumbled upon the desire that—in Fineman's formulation— arises in response to "anecdotal form." In "The History of the Anecdote," the moment desire arises is not just the content of a particular anecdote but has a necessary, "characteristic" relation to anecdote itself. In light of Fineman's theorization, I can see "Knot a Love Story" as an exploration of anecdotal desire.

The specific desire examined in "Knot a Love Story" is pedagogical: the essay tells of my falling in love with a graduate student. An incident with a graduate student is likewise at the origin of the next essay in part 2. Just a few weeks after writing "Knot," I was teaching a graduate course and found myself using all my ingenuity to produce a reading that would impress Ellen sitting directly across the seminar table from me.

The text for the day was Derrida's *Spurs*. It was Ellen's turn to give an oral presentation; the first half of class would be devoted to her reading of the text. The second half of class was my responsibility: although I had read *Spurs* a good number of times, I came up with a reading that had never occurred to me before. While preparing for class, I was vaguely aware that I was performing this reading "for Ellen."

Ellen's oral presentation was dazzling; I was delighted; she also clearly liked my reading. During class, as Ellen and I played with Derrida's words and ideas, egging each other on in high theoretical wordplay, I became giddy. I remember at one point I just could not stop laughing, could no longer speak. I don't think I've ever let myself get carried away in the classroom to that extent—so much, so pleasurably, so productively.

A couple weeks later, Ellen was sitting in my office during office hours; the phone rang—it was someone asking if I would contribute to an anthology on Derrida and feminism. I turned to Ellen and told her what I was being asked, and she encouraged me to write up the reading I had done in class for inclusion in the anthology. Ellen's presence there at the moment of this call felt like a meaningful coincidence; I said yes to the woman on the phone. I made my decision because Ellen was there, because she wanted me to do it. If not for Ellen, I would not have produced this reading; if not for her presence at that moment, I would not have written this essay.

Located at the juncture of theorizing and pedagogical passion, the third essay in part 2 is thus anecdotally close to "Knot a Love Story." Theoretically, however, it is closer to "A Tale of Two Jacques." Returning to a 1970s text by Derrida, another text that was crucial to my intellectual formation in graduate school, the third essay—like "A Tale"—tries to look back on Derrida's text from the vantage point of the nineties. "Dating Derrida in the Nineties," however, succeeds where the first attempt failed. Where "Two Jacques" compulsively marked time but failed to achieve a theoretical perspective, "Dating Derrida" embraces the marking of time as a theoretical perspective.

Reading the inscription of "72" in this 1972 text along with the use of the phrase "faire époque" [marks an era], I find Derrida marking the moment of his writing. "Dating Derrida" concludes: "Derrida took pains to date his text and I want to read rather than erase those marks." Reading those marks is part of what the title calls "dating." While I relish how the word flirts with the anecdotal erotics that tie this essay to "Knot a Love Story," "dating" is here primarily about registering temporality, and explicitly connected to history.

"Dating Derrida in the Nineties" brings an explicit concern with history into the conception of anecdotal theory. The anecdote has everything to do with history: as an account of an actual incident, it is, as Fineman puts it (67), "the smallest minimal unit" of historiography. Small though it may be, anecdote has major historical effect: it is, according to Fineman, "the opening of history that lets history happen" (73).

Fineman's discussion of anecdotal opening and teleological narration is in fact actually about history. While anecdote is the opening to history, anecdotes are characteristically embedded in larger, overarching histories. The teleological drive tends to make those larger histories, ironically, ahistorical:

> Properly speaking such a history is not historical. Governed by an . . . inexorable teleological unfolding . . . every moment . . . is thereby rendered timeless: such moments . . . exist . . . outside of time . . . because their momentary durative appearance is already but the guaranteed foreshadow, the already all but realized promise of the concluding end . . . towards which tendentiously, as but the passing moments in a story whose conclusion is already written, they tend. (68)

If there is one narrative which has even stronger teleological tendencies than the love story, it is definitely the writing of history.

My project of dating theory is about locating theory in the moment and is thus a historical project. However, as Fineman suggests, the historical project tends to lose the moment in pursuit of grander meaning. And in that pursuit, rather than making theory accountable to the play of event, we are more likely to find ourselves producing histories governed by our timeless theories.[1] Because I do indeed want to open theory to history, to the unforeseenness of temporal existence, I would term my project an attempt not to historicize but to anecdotalize theory. While the anecdotal is indeed historical, its focus is on the singular moment. I share Fineman's sense that "the opening of history occurs for but a moment" (75).

In 1992, when I wrote "Dating Derrida," the reigning theoretical perspective in both feminist and literary theory was in fact historicist. The reading of Derrida in the essay is very much in keeping with that nineties theoretical paradigm. However, beyond the dominant historicism, the essay also broaches another relation to history: not only must we historicize our objects of study, but we must face what I there call "our own embedding in history." In "Dating Derrida," this second relation to history—beyond the historicist reading of the text—is anecdotal.

While historicist readings of texts were very much in the air in 1992, "Dating Derrida in the Nineties" also dates that air itself, historicizing not only the object of study but also the subject, the scholarly perspective.[2] This other historicism manifests itself as the story of Ellen, which fuels and frames my reading. In and through that anecdote, the essay historicizes the subject of knowledge, exploring our subjective relation to history.

In "Dating Derrida," that subjective relation to history is, in a word, "anxious": "The critique of our [essentialism] has led us to historicize but has not made us less anxious about our own embedding in history. . . . We cannot be endlessly up-to-date." If "dating" figures the historicism of this 1992 essay, this other, subjective historicism appears as the anxiety of being dated.

The anxious relation to history here recalls the anxiety in "A Tale of Two Jacques." The two anxieties have more in common than may first appear. Bringing "Dating"'s explicitly historical perspective to bear on the earlier essay, we could come to understand the anxiety in "Jacques" as an encounter with this same subjective relation to history. This anxious historicism—enacted in "Jacques," theorized in "Derrida"—is not just a look at the past from our perspective in the present but the fear that we ourselves might be stuck in the past.

■　■　■

I delivered "A Tale of Two Jacques" at the 1991 MLA convention in San Francisco; the talk was about going back to places I had been before. Seven years later I was back in San Francisco giving a talk at the MLA entitled "Castration Anxiety and the Unemployed Ph.D." That paper is the fourth essay in part 2.

Like "Jacques," this 1998 paper uses psychoanalytic theory and begins by recounting an experience I had in the mid-1970s. The relation between theory and story in the two texts is, however, reversed. In 1991 I was expected to do psychoanalytic theory but instead found myself telling stories; in 1998 I was in fact invited to tell stories (the MLA session was entitled "Tales from the Job Front") and felt somewhat transgressive doing psychoanalytic theory in my talk.

In 1991 I experienced anxiety at finding myself mired in the anecdotal, unable to attain theoretical perspective; in 1998 I theorized about anxiety, confidently moving back and forth between anecdotal and theoretical discourse. The contrast between these two MLA papers (the two shortest pieces in this collection) makes clear the distance my anecdotal theorizing traveled from the beginning to the end of the decade. While the first three essays in part 2—written in the same nine-month period—together represent the gestation of anecdotal theory, the last two essays represent an anecdotal theory sure of itself and its claims to theoretical and practical value.

Although a short piece, "Castration Anxiety" makes large claims for the theoretical value of telling stories. It questions the tendency of literary scholars to deal with important issues by turning to theoretical discourses based in other academic disciplines like sociology and economics. It proposes instead that we theorize based in what we know best, in what we know professionally. "Castration Anxiety and the Unemployed Ph.D." argues for a more literary theory.

Nine months after "Castration Anxiety," I wrote the last essay in part 2. I began this preface by suggesting that the marks of time in that final piece are more precise than in the earlier essays, the emphasis on the moment even greater. Written late in 1999, "Econstructing Sisterhood" in fact represents the extremity of marking time in *Anecdotal Theory*. In keeping with the project of subjective historicism, the time marked in "Econstructing" is the temporality of its own theorizing.

"9/27/99, at 6:32 P.M., I wrote Judi . . . 'I'm trying to write an ending to EcoSis.'" This sentence from "Econstructing Sisterhood" quotes an email I wrote my sister while at work on the paper (which I refer to by abbreviated nickname). Email provides a record not only of the date but of the hour and minute. This is the only point in the essay—indeed in the whole volume—where the registering of time progresses from calendar to clock time. It seems worth noting that this most extreme mark of time appears at the moment I feel the lack of and long for a conclusion. This suggests there might be some connection between the teleological yearning for a conclusion and the urge to capture the moment. Perhaps it is that the ultimate capture would arrest time, stop it and bring it to an end.

At 7:18 P.M. that same evening Judi sent a response to my email which, it turns out, provided me with a text I used in my conclusion. Using that text in the conclusion involved narrating the email exchange where it arose. In place of a theoretical conclusion, "Econstructing Sisterhood" tells the anecdote of my need for a conclusion.

Although what my sister sent provided the conclusion for "Econstructing" as a talk, the essay does not end there. Several pages of afterword follow. This final essay of *Anecdotal Theory*—though powerfully drawn toward closure—reopens, more than once . . . actually ending with a declaration of its suspicion of teleology ("this seems too cozy an ending") . . . ending finally with the promise of another story . . .

In the fall of 1974, I heard that Derrida was to lecture on Lacan in Buffalo. I drove the four hours from Ithaca to Buffalo, frantically looked for the building on a campus I didn't know, arrived after Derrida had begun, finding a seat way back in the balcony. In that already distracted state, I had a lot of trouble following the lecture, but it nonetheless threw me into a defensive panic. Derrida was saying terrible things about Lacan.

About six months later "Le Facteur de la vérité" came out in *Poetique.* Getting a hold of it as soon as possible, I read it and found myself in a state. I had to write something, had to counteract Derrida's text. I intently queried everyone I knew who read "Le Facteur," hoping they could see that Derrida was wrong. Nothing I have read ever worked me up as much, not even negative reviews of my own books. Never have I felt so strongly: "I must write something to fix this." I never did write that retort, but sometimes I think that all my writing for the next decade was a displaced version of it.

Derrida came to America and called Lacan phallocentric. Actually he called him "phallogocentric," but the part about the logos didn't bother me much. When I heard Derrida call Lacan phallocentric, I felt as if Derrida had castrated Lacan, as if he had taken away Lacan's phallus and/or revealed his lack. I have read that certain male-identified women defend militantly against the recognition of their father's castration[1]—a female form of castration anxiety.

A year after reading "Le Facteur de la vérité" I wrote, in an article called "The Ladies' Man": "If any writing equals Lacan's . . . it is Derrida's. Both are at once extremely forceful (masculine) and maddeningly sneaky (feminine). Doubtless the battle between these two intellectual superstars, flaunting their masculinity *and* femininity, is too sexy—too uncannily staging the battle of the sexes—for either ever to be declared the hands-off winner. However . . . one solid accusation comes through Derrida's sinuous exposition. . . . Lacan stands accused of . . . 'phallogocentrism.' "[2]

A decade ago, revising "The Ladies' Man" for inclusion in *The Daughter's Seduction,* such lines were an embarrassment to me and I had the good sense to excise them. I return to them now because they are a record of my attempt to repair what I experienced as Derrida's castration of Lacan. Following the crude gendering in this passage, "one solid accusation comes through Derrida's sinuous exposition" implies that despite the veil of "feminine" sinuosity, we can see the "masculine" solid; I am attempting to unveil Derrida's masculinity. It would seem that, in a cultural feminist reversal, the feminine terms are privileged; masculinity is lack. But in this entire lurid passage, the only italicized word is the "and" in the phrase "masculinity *and* femininity." What makes the stars "super" is neither masculinity nor femininity but the "and." Accusing Lacan of phallocentrism, Derrida reduces him to simple masculinity and thus castrates him of his "and."

I felt as if Derrida had the phallus which Lacan lacked and I wanted to take it from Derrida, but castrating Derrida could not restore Lacan's phallus. I try to even the score by proving Derrida masculine, i.e., phallocentric, but at the same time I also try to construct Lacan and Derrida as a heterosexual couple and eroticize their opposition: thus I refer to "the battle of the sexes" to suggest the quarrel is some sort of conjugal argument. The hope that neither will be declared "the hands-off winner" seems to carry the wish that the battle will go on and they will keep touching each other.

My graduate education had reconstructed me as a daughter of Derrida and Lacan. I understood and valued each in relation to and through the other; I had an investment in Lacan *and* Derrida, emphasis on the "and."[3] Derrida's critique of Lacan made me feel like the child of divorcing parents; if they were opposed, then I had to choose; if I had to choose, then I had to lose. My desperation to bring them together set me against one of them as he insisted upon articulating their differences. Through my panic I could not help but see that they were indeed not together; I could not both bring them together and be where they were; we could not all three be together.

Sometime in 1978 I read Barbara Johnson's "The Frame of Reference" in *Yale French Studies* and found a sister. Acknowledging Lacan and Derrida as parents, her article looks unflinchingly at their quarrel, sides with neither, and, without at all denying their opposition, brings them together, reinscribing the opposition within a "round robin," a game of taking turns.[4] Split by Derrida's critique, I felt repaired by Johnson and immensely relieved.

■ ■ ■

Last March I finished a book I had been working on for some six years, a book on American feminist criticism. As I was putting finishing touches on the afterword of that book, I got a phone call from Ned Lukacher, inviting me to present a paper in an MLA session on "Lacan and Derrida Revisited." The timing seemed perfect: finishing a project, I was wondering what to do next; after concentrating on American women, I wondered what it would be like to go back and "revisit" two figures who had been so central to my earlier work.

That night I had a dream or, as the French say, I "made a dream": I'm standing in a small, pleasant body of water, playing with my boyfriend (Dick) and our son (Max). We're taking turns making up a song about small water animals, each in turn making up a verse about a different animal, getting our inspiration from animals we see. I see first one then two frogs emerge from the water and I (or someone) make a verse about them. Suddenly I see something hairy (furry), too big to be a frog, beginning to surface. I can see through the water that it is quite big; I'm afraid because I have no idea what it is. I ask Dick what it is, but he keeps looking in the wrong direction and not seeing it. He only sees the two frogs (who are still there) and says, "it's a frog." Then I notice a second of these big, furry creatures appearing on the other side of Dick (who is standing opposite me). (By this time, Max has disappeared from the dream—there are just me, two bullfrogs, Dick, and these two large furry creatures.) Dick finally seems to see the first of the creatures, and I realize, to my horror, that he doesn't know what it is either. I can't move to get away; I scream and wake myself up. I lie awake in bed, shaken, thinking about the dream. About fifteen minutes later, remembering Ned's phone call, I say to myself "two big hairy frogs," get up, and write down the dream.

Six months later, rereading "Le Facteur de la vérité" in preparation for writing this paper, Derrida's discussion of Lacan reminded me of this dream. The more I read the more connections I made, until I began to feel that the dream itself was some sort of reading of "Le Facteur." A fantasy: an interpretation of dreams where dreams interpret theory rather than vice versa. A fantasy? or maybe we could call it psychoanalytic theory?

The dream begins on an unusually pleasant family scene: the Oedipal triangle become a game of taking turns. Lacan's "Seminar" identifies three positions in Poe's "The Purloined Letter" and shows that a character can, in turn, go from one position to the other, as the letter passes from hand to hand. Derrida identifies Lacan's structural triangles as "Oedipal" and also emphasizes how each individual in turn occupies each of the positions: the Oedipal triangle as a "round robin," a pleasant familial game of turns. Barbara Johnson expands the frame to show how Lacan and Derrida follow Poe's characters, in turn, from one position to the other.

Derrida emphasizes the triadic configurations because he wants to point out that Lacan's fascination with the triangles excludes consideration of certain kinds of dyads. Demonstrating various manifestations of doubles and doubling in Poe's story, Derrida writes: "If Dupin is double in himself, and if he is the double of a double (the narrator), etc., this threatens to introduce a certain perturbation in the delimitation of the triangles."[5] The double, or rather the uncannily redoubling doubles, "threatens to introduce a certain perturbation" in the triangular family game. In the nightmare, the ludic Oedipal is disturbed by two identical uncanny creatures who are confused with two identical frogs; once these double doubles are introduced, Max disappears from the original threesome, reducing us to a pair.

Conventionally, the Lacanian, Freudian Oedipal interrupts an idyllic pre-Oedipal dyad, an illusory, pleasurable, safe space of familial indifferentiation; the triangular symbolic disrupts the dyadic imaginary. In this dream, however, the original idyllic configuration is triadic and is interrupted by proliferating pairs. Quoting from Derrida, the same passage: "The Seminar mercilessly forecloses this problematic of the double and of the *Unheimlichkeit*. No doubt considering that it is contained in the imaginary, in the dual relation which must be rigorously kept apart from the symbolic and the triangular." The verb "forecloses" is Lacan's term for an absolute and psychotic exclusion of the Oedipal third term, of the triangular symbolic. Derrida's use of it here suggests a certain reversal whereby the delusory safety of the triangular is maintained by the defensive exclusion of a certain threatening dyadic.

Yet it is not actually a simple reversal, two now coming after three. The dream doubles one initial frog, and then redoubles with another pair of creatures, at the same time reducing the original comfy threesome to an anxious pair. "If Dupin is double in himself, and if he is the double of a double, etc., this threatens to introduce a certain perturbation." There is a doubling of doubles, and there is also the "etc." Johnson comments: "If the doubles are forever redividing or multiplying, does the number '2' really apply?"[6]

Derrida on Lacan, the same passage, again: "What thus finds itself controlled, is the *Unheimlichkeit*, and the anxious panic that can be provoked by . . . the relays . . . from double to double. . . . By neutralizing the double, the Seminar does everything necessary to avoid what [Lacan elsewhere] calls 'unmasterable anxiety.' "

The last time I visited Lacan and Derrida, around 1981, I quoted this same last sentence, commenting that Derrida "accuses [Lacan] of avoiding and repressing manifestations of the double." I went on to say there, "But one could likewise say that Derrida . . . [is] avoiding some anxiety-producing double," thus myself trying to put one Jacques in the place of the other, trying to control my anxiety through pairing Jacques. I went on to close my chapter "The American Other" with a rousing, hortatory "we must risk the anxiety of the double."[7]

■ ■ ■

What is the relation between "the anxiety of the double" and castration anxiety? Freud's essay "The Uncanny," his reading of Hoffmann's "The Sand-Man," considers them both. Derrida would have it that a psychoanalytic obsession with castration does not do justice to "the anxiety of the double." I would like to know how the two interact.[8]

My anxiety dream is not without reference to castration. As the dream begins, I am secure in the supposition of Dick's knowledge: he is supposed to know what the creatures are. First he cannot see; then he sees but does not know. My panic is unleashed not by the sight of the hairy creatures but by the revelation of Dick's lack (so to speak).

If Dick too does not know, then rather than my complement he is my double. I also experienced Barbara Johnson as a double, but that double reassured me; in that case the double had what I lack. In understanding this contrast, I think first, necessarily, of gender: same, different, male, female. But that does not seem satisfactory. Alternatively I consider the factor of mastery. It's a pleasure to identify with someone who has it under control; what Lacan and Derrida call "unmasterable anxiety" occurs when we identify with someone who ought to know but is himself anxious.

It is as if the dream were a reversal of the scene from my past. Johnson's essay transformed the threat of two big bullfrogs into a pleasant game; the dream starts with the round robin and plunges me back into double anxiety.

■ ■ ■

In agreeing to write this paper, I imagined revisiting the battlefield of an old dead anxiety and feeling triumph. And I fantasized that as someone who no longer has a strong stake in Lacan or Derrida, I would have clear-sighted wisdom, cool recollection to offer from my vantage of beyond. Instead I got anxious, not only in my dream, but as I wrote this paper or rather as I resisted writing this paper, resisted really getting into Lacan and Derrida again, reopening that can of worms.

Lacan and Derrida "revisited" suggests a certain mapping of memory, one in which we go back to a place we have been before. Two big frogs emerging from the depths implies a different config-uration, where something comes back to us—figures return from the past to disturb an idyllic present, aliens threatening domestic security—a classic scenic representation of Freudian "depth psy-chology," the return of the repressed: Lacan and Derrida revisit*ing*.

Half a dozen years ago, new to Rice University and anxious to find students to work with, I agreed to an independent study that a graduate student proposed. We would meet for half an hour once every two weeks; he would read psychoanalytic theory and write six short papers. Readings were structured around my undergraduate course on Freud and my just published book on Lacan, so that this supplementary course would not demand much time or effort on my part. Commuting weekly from home in Milwaukee to Rice in Houston, trying to get my next book done, although I wanted students, in fact I had little time to give them.

A few weeks into the semester the student turned in his first paper as I was off to the airport for my Thursday evening commute. Reading it on the plane, I couldn't see what he was trying to say; so, disappointed, I gave it a B-. Back at Rice on Tuesday morning, I put it in his mailbox so he would have time to read my comments before we met that afternoon. Over the weekend—through research time, social life, and family time—I had in fact completely forgotten about the grade, so I was at first puzzled when he showed up in my office the next day, obviously agitated.

I could see agitation, but it was only later I learned how angry he actually was. In retrospect I recognize that graduate students usually are offended by a B-, but trying to fulfill my teaching duties despite an impossibly busy schedule meant I got the work done (preparation, grading, advising) but didn't have time to reflect on its effects. He walked into my office and demanded to know—in a hyper-controlled voice through which a certain shaking nonetheless appeared—what I was doing. I didn't know what he was talking about. He asked point-blank why I had given him a B-. Then I remembered and replied that that is the grade I give to papers where the writing is so bad I don't understand the point. Recognizing one of those never pleasant situations when a student protests his grade, I braced myself to stand my ground.

After a few back and forths between his challenge and my reiterated position, he asked if we could read through the paper together. I resisted: that would take hours. He stood by his demand; my resistance fixed upon the time it would take, time I did not have. Finally, as a way out of deadlock, I agreed to begin going through the paper, thinking that beginning would demonstrate how impossible his demand was, how much time it would take. I know now that he believed if he could get me actually to read the paper with him I would be confronted with its excellence and forced to recognize my error.

So we began—with adversarially opposed agendas. I would read a sentence aloud, then say what I understood and indicate portions I did not understand. He then would explain what he had been trying to say. This was, as I had imagined, a very time-consuming activity: the full discussion of a sentence took ten minutes or so; in the half hour allotted to our meeting we had gotten through the first paragraph.

At first this exchange had quite a bite; underlying the discussion were mutual accusations of blindness. As I indicated what I didn't get, it was as if to say: "See, your writing fails, you deserve a B-." When he explained what he meant, it was as much as saying: "This is so obviously a worthy and interesting idea; you are prejudiced, stupid, or crazy if you can't see that." But, by the time we had gotten through the first paragraph, something had changed. We were no longer fighting each other; we were in fact working together.

In retrospect, I am amazed that he could give up not only his challenge but the sort of defensiveness a writer usually exhibits in discussion of his less than successful writing. He had moved from trying to "show" me to trying to see the paper as I saw it. The going was slow and difficult, but there were little breakthroughs. I would come to understand what he had been trying to say; he would realize how and why the sentence did not communicate what he thought it meant. Progressing sentence by sentence, each now working hard to explain or grasp, we moved slowly but thoroughly through the text with what seemed a shared double understanding: of what he had been trying to say and of what the paper actually said.

This painstaking work, the sense of laboring together and building understanding, was enormously satisfying and totally engrossing. Partway through the second page, I realized an hour had gone by; it was 5:30. I called the friend I was to meet for dinner at six, told her something had come up and asked if we could reschedule. Looking back, that phone call (and the decision behind it) feels like some sort of turning point. My resistance had specifically focused on how much time he was demanding; this commitment to pursue to the end of the paper represented a dramatic giving up of that resistance. When I phoned my friend, I was giving the student what he had demanded, but now I too wanted this.

At seven P.M., after two and a half hours, we reached the end of the paper, neither until then letting up concentration, the concerted effort to understand and communicate. We were both exhausted, but I for one felt a pleasure in that. He seemed overwhelmed and silenced. He had gotten what he demanded—my full attention and explanation—but the angry young man who had walked in challenging my judgment had come to see the paper as I did, as a B-paper, in graduate school terms, a failure. He sat there huddled over and seemed very vulnerable. I wanted to comfort and reassure him, imagined patting him on the head. What I did was lean over so I was actually looking up at his lowered head in order to make eye contact. He was amused and, I believe, lifted from his despond.

Since we had not had a chance to discuss the readings, I offered to meet again for a half hour on Thursday. We agreed upon a time and parted. I went home, had a drink, and ate dinner in a strangely agitated state. Unable to concentrate on anything, I retreated into TV watching and then sleep. Normally an extremely sound sleeper, I woke up in the middle of the night, agitated, thinking about this student, about the extraordinary time passed in my office. Unable to fall back to sleep, I turned my energy to grading a batch of papers from my undergraduate Freud class, allowing me to return them earlier than I had promised. I felt, excitedly, like a really good teacher, finding unsuspected pockets of time for my students.

All the next day, I thought of the graduate student, obsessively. By afternoon, these thoughts had become recognizably erotic. By Thursday I suspected I had a crush on him and began to talk about it with friends, feeling the need for help in dealing with this. My obsessive thoughts, my sexual fantasizing, were real sources of pleasure, but within a few days I went from feeling like a wonderful teacher to feeling myself a very bad teacher indeed.

As well as I can judge, I was both. He learned in that session to see his writing more clearly, to recognize when it did not say what he wanted it to. His writing improved steadily: his next paper earned an A-; by the end of the semester he was writing excellent papers. I continued to devote time to meeting with him and was particularly eager to go over his writing, trying in fact to reproduce that extraordinarily pleasurable experience. My desire for him also grew steadily: by the end of the semester I felt as if I were in love.

I am in fact convinced that not only was I both a good and a bad teacher (by most any standard I am aware of for such evaluations), but that I became both at one and the same time, in one and the same move—in that moment when I called my friend to cancel dinner, when I decided to give him the time he needed but also when I wanted to stay with him until we finished. I suspect that what made me a good teacher was precisely what made me a bad teacher.

It is this apparent paradox that I propose to examine in this essay. I do not use the word "paradox" blithely here; it marks an experience of nearly unbearable ethical conflict as my psyche swung between a manic sense of my beneficent power and a horrifying image of myself as dirty old lech. I was aroused in fact by the sense that I was a "good teacher," by feeling my power to help someone reach his fullest. Yet the arousal meant I was getting off on being his teacher, using him for my own perverse gratification. Although I have felt the weight of that paradox tear at my affects and my self-esteem, I term the paradox "apparent" in the hope of rethinking our pedagogical morality.

In deciding to write and publish this essay, I am wagering that I am not a pervert, that this incident, although perhaps clearer and more dramatic, is in its ambiguity fairly representative of a broad range of pedagogical experience. The remainder of the essay will attempt to work through this incident, to analyze what happened and why, and to articulate some of the theoretical questions posed by it. But before going on to that work, out of consideration for the reader I should negotiate the dissolution of our implicit narrative pact. This is not a love story, rather a story of falling in love. Narrative convention leads us to take "falling in love" as the opening scene of a drama which will unfold so as to determine whether that scene should be, retrospectively, interpreted as "love" or "fall," or even, most compellingly, as both. Here, however, it is not the opening scene but the whole story. Recounting it, I feel the pull toward conventional closure: did we do it? what happened? Half a dozen years ago, living the story, I felt—much more powerfully—the same pull: felt impelled against my better judgment to push for consummation or rejection. But in fact, from the point of view of narrative promise, "nothing happened": we neither had sex nor damaged our pedagogical relation.

My urge—as reader, writer, or protagonist—to turn this into a love story is massive. Whether the story then had a happy or disastrous ending, it would in any case remove us from the scene of pedagogy, would definitively interpret what happened not as teaching but as love. Yet the tale I need to tell—from grade protest to the full bloom of my crush—is a story of desire arising within the scene of pedagogy, where it is troublingly unclear whether this is really teaching or really sex. Narrative convention directs us to decide whether this story belongs to romance or accounts of teaching experience. To make that generic decision is also to decide whether I was a good or a bad teacher: the good teacher could conquer this and put it to pedagogical use; the bad teacher would give in to desire and abandon duty.

The pressure to decide whether the scene belongs to romance or to professional experience asserts itself not only in the drive to find out how it ended, but also in the stylistics of my account. Some of the language, the agitation, the not-realizing-until-later, the rhythm, clearly derive from romantic convention. Other portions of the account, the stress on labor, words like "communicate" and "understand," seem to derive from the equally conventional discourse of the good teacher. Not only are there two different discursive styles, but the narrating subject is temporally split; two narrative points of view interlace: what I experienced then and what I know now. This temporal splitting of the first-person narrator can be heard in two voices: the voice of the romantic heroine—impelled by the story, not knowing what will happen—and the older but wiser teacherly voice—not only a knowing subject but she who transforms experience into lesson.

Writing and rereading the narrative, I find myself embarrassed not, as I had imagined, by the romantic confession, but much more by the "goody-goody," naively idealistic language of the teacherly voice. Readerly pleasure pulls toward the romantic interpretation. The only language I can summon to describe a powerful experience of doing exactly what I imagine to be good teaching seems bankrupt. Perhaps recognizably conventional discourse seems more appropriate for an impelled, ignorant heroine, more foolish for a knowing, teaching subject. But I also suspect that my preference for romantic over pedagogical cliché is knotted to my persistent urge to interpret this experience and this relation as erotic rather than professional, as love story rather than teaching experience.

■　■　■

For months, whenever I thought about those hours in my office, it was like remembering going to bed with someone. I felt we had shared something intense and intimate, that during that time I was totally focused, totally there with him. I found myself speaking of that session in embarrassed, excited, inadequate periphrasis. In memory, the scene became deeply eroticized: by that I do not mean that I revised it with sexual content (touching or innuendo), but the memory had an aura of treasure around it. Thinking about my relation to this student, I began to refer to that afternoon in my office as "the primal scene."

"Primal" because it felt like some sort of origin point. In two decades of teaching, I have had various intense relations with students: friendships, enmities, even—in my younger, wilder days— actual affairs. I choose to consider this scene, not because the relation is unique, but because the scene is unique. Of all the various ambiguous and charged relations with students, this is the only one where I feel I can locate the beginning of my erotic investment. Into my office that afternoon walked a student with an obvious interest in working with me to whom I gave little thought; when he walked out two and a half hours later, he had moved to the center of my thoughts, where he stayed for many months. Because this event has for me something like the magical status of an origin, I persist in believing (despite familiarity with the technique for "deconstructing" origins) that if I could analyze this event I would understand how and why I invest erotically in students.

Because I have a fix on where this cathexis arose, I feel certain, in a way I cannot be about any other of my relations with students, that the erotic charge arose not alongside of the pedagogical relation (not coincidentally because I liked X body type or Y personality or because Z was going on in my psychosexual life), but that the desire arose as part and parcel of a scene of pedagogy. The eros was not a deviation, a distraction, an addition, an aside; it arose in the center of what was a purely pedagogical exchange, as pure as any such can be.

What precisely was so erotic about the scene that had taken place in my office? Recalling it for this account, I am struck by the drama of resistance and vulnerability. The backdrop of his initial anger and challenge give particular piquancy to my sense of his placing himself, undefended and vulnerable, in my hands, trusting it would do him good. I feel as if he let me put his balls in my mouth.

As this image makes clear, eros here is tied to gender. Both the anger against which I stand my ground and the vulnerability that so moves me are gendered masculine in my account. The transformation of masculine threat into male vulnerability is certainly part of the pleasure: what might be understood as a turn from figurative "balls" to corporeal ones.

This drama of resistance and subsequent capitulation, fantasy resolution of the battle of the sexes, is the most sensational representation of the eros; it's what strikes my fancy, what I prefer to imagine and recount. What happened after he ceased resisting, after I too gave up my resistance, is less dramatic, less sexy to recount, to imagine, but is in fact where not only the teaching but also "the sex" happened. The intimacy of working together without barriers between us was, I believe, the sensation I desired to repeat, was the experience that felt like sex. But it is also what occasions the goody-goody prose and is in imagination or in the telling not erotic. Something about erotic representation pushes me toward locating the eros in the power struggle, which is its necessary but not sufficient precondition. In the narrative, what happens when the power struggle is over seems prissy, teacherly. But I do believe that what aroused me in the scene was this moment when we were being good together and not—as imagination would recount—a hot, bad drama of violence and power.

While that intimate experience of being good together seems to have little to do with gender, the preliminary battle and the fantasy repetitions that insistently frame that experience are hypergendered. Whether in my idealistic utopian mode or in my bad-girl fantasies, I would like to separate and choose one of these erotics and discard the other. But to my embarrassment I find I cannot disentangle an erotic which I believe to be gender-irrelevant from hypergendered scenarios. I thus find myself in the apparently contradictory position of claiming this scene as generally representative of pedagogical relations, regardless of gender, while at the same time emphasizing the particular gendering of female teacher and male student.

This contradictory position impels me to attempt to disentangle the two, but I nonetheless say "apparently contradictory" out of an inkling that the specific gender configuration here may actually help make the scene generally representative. Although I have in fact had more fantasies about, sex with, crushes on, female students than male students, I have chosen here to look at this scene because I suspect the particular gendering of female teacher and male student makes it possible to see an erotic play of pedagogy that is usually overlaid by oppressively real power relations. Here gender hierarchy crosses pedagogical position: teacher's power runs counter to male prerogative. The contradiction between the two hierarchies destabilizes the positions, makes each position seem, at least in part, play-acting.

I used to play school when I was a child, after I had started going to the real one. I would play with my brother, my only younger sibling, who was not yet himself in school. During those games where I was always the teacher, I believe I really taught him to read.

I go back to my infantile pedagogy because I imagine it tells something about why and how I wanted to be a teacher. Probably most teachers who care about teaching, probably many who are good teachers, wanted to be teachers. And behind the guidance counselor's phrasing, we might recognize something like the drive to be the teacher, the teacher's desire.

The phrase "infantile pedagogy" is meant to allude to the Freudian notion of "infantile sexuality." Freud thought that in order to understand what we usually call sexuality, we must recognize its first flowering in childhood. Adult sexuality takes its shape and its force by being an unconscious—and therefore conflicted and contorted—

repetition of certain childhood relations and configurations. I am suggesting, analogously, that to understand (adult) teaching, we might posit it as a conflicted and contorted repetition of certain childhood configurations. I am not saying that playing school with my brother was sexual but that the repetition of the infantile in the adult activity sexualizes the latter.

Going back to my own childhood, I hope to understand things of wider application than just to those teachers who started out as big sisters instructing their little brothers. In proposing the concept of infantile pedagogy, I am imagining that teaching in general is informed by largely unconscious reactivations of powerful childhood pedagogical configurations, which, of course, in their specific forms vary with the individual.

Fifteen years after playing school with my brother, I started to teach "for real." My last year of graduate school, I taught my first (and second) class: the same course both semesters, but the second semester one student became particularly interested in things I was saying about the books we were reading; one young man wanted to learn what I wanted to teach. We started meeting for coffee and talk outside of class. I began to burn with desire for him, applied my wits to seducing him, and—although I got nowhere sexually—we had a lot of great conversations.

Mike was smart and good-looking but I don't believe that's what led me to chase him all over campus. What overheated me was the fit between some fantasy I had and the way he responded to me. It is probably very much to the point that I was at the time still a student, with my own very strong cathexes onto teachers. Mike took me for a teacher and appeared to be learning from me in the very way I was still learning from my teachers. I remember often thinking that he must be the same age as my brother: I was still "playing teacher."

In relation to Mike, I was not only playing the teacher but was specifically playing my teachers, my dissertation committee, who were all male. In this fantasylike reversal, Mike was not the student, but was me as student. The positions that I thought of as real were me-female-student and my male teachers. In this seeming reality, gender and pedagogical hierarchy relayed each other and I could not disentangle the one who had the knowledge from the one who had the balls. Finding myself in an analogous relation to Mike but in the opposite role, I felt I had switched genders. My concurrent sense of our "real genders," however, caused me to experience the peda-gogical positions as drag performance, role-playing.

Although "being the teacher" felt like a masquerade, I am con-vinced that Mike learned a lot from me. An academic himself today, he supports this sense of the real pedagogical value of our encoun-ter. This ambiguity between play and real teaching goes back beyond Mike to my infantile pedagogy. I believe I actually did teach my brother to read. Both of these primal scenes take on formative force precisely by combining playing teacher with really teaching. The fantasy sense of being in a role that was not by rights mine made me feel very powerful, but it is the apparent "real" effect of the game which was so totally intoxicating. This knot of pretense and reality is, I believe, the very paradoxical heart of my pedagogy. I was, and from the beginning, at one and the same time, a fake teacher and an effective one. I am—after twenty years of teaching literally hundreds of students, as a "full professor"—still getting off on "playing teach-er" even or especially while I actually teach.

■   ■   ■

As I work my way through this material, it keeps organizing itself into opposed pairs: teaching/sex, understanding/conflict, duty/gratification, experience/representation, gender-blind/hyper-gen-dered, reality/pretense, labor/play. A strong moralizing impulse would reduce each pair to the opposition between good and bad, demand we separate them and choose. But not just the moralizing impulse. My erotic fantasies, my romantic daydreams, and my nar-rative pleasure would likewise also disentangle the two strands. My wish to be good and my fantasy of being bad would both claim one strand and disavow the other. These impulses to separate are radi-cal: the strands represent competing interpretations of the scene, of self, of life. But, working my way through the material of this scene, over and over, I sense that these strands are inextricably entangled.

One more opposed pair of terms before I close, this one, in the actuality of writing this essay, the most troubling: theory and story. What I wanted to do in this essay was tell this story; to justify that, I felt it must do a lot of theoretical work. Throughout this writing, I have feared that there is too much story, at the same time as I found myself continually falling back into story, adding more stories in the latter part which is supposed to be theory. If story is not subordinate to theory, then I have fallen short of duty, given in to my own (exhibitionist) gratification.

The protagonist of this essay fantasized and feared betraying her identity as teacher, but by the time I chose to write this up, I knew the outcome and was pretty confident I had maintained my identity. But the drama of professional identity repeats itself in the scene of writing. Choosing to write this for a professional journal meant worrying about whether the writing is professional, scholarly, academic. Although the dry, negative connotations of those terms urge me to transgress and disavow this identity, my choice of this context signifies a wish this essay be taken as writing that serves the pursuit of knowledge. Although I do not like writing with a teacherly voice, to be included in this professional journal this writing ought to turn life to lesson for more general application (for the benefit of others), to subordinate story to theory.

On the level of greatest actuality, in today's scene of writing rather than the pedagogical scene from my past, the real moral knot, the question that tears me is not about falling in love but about falling into story, not whether or not this is a love story, but whether or not this is a story.

Derrida first presented the paper I will call *Spurs* at the 1972 symposium entitled "Nietzsche Today?"[1] Derrida interpreted the second word of the symposium title by choosing to speak on Nietzsche and women. "La 'femme'—le mot fait époque," Derrida says in 1972 (60). The French expression "faire époque," my French-English dictionary tells me, can be rendered by the English expression "marks an era." The era marked by the word "woman" was the today in which Derrida speaks.

A generation ago, Derrida began his talk with a dateline: "From Basel in seventy-two (*The Birth of Tragedy*) Nietzsche writes to Malvida von Meysenbug" (35). These are the very first words of *Spurs*. Derrida goes on to quote a few sentences from Nietzsche's 1872 letter to von Meysenbug as a sort of epigraph, what he and his American translator call an "exergue." An "exergue," my English dictionary informs me, is "a space on a coin, token, or medal . . . often containing the date." Speaking in 1972 at a conference on "Nietzsche Today?" Derrida casually dates Nietzsche's letter as "seventy-two," taking to heart the question "Today?" in his assignment to talk about Nietzsche. Twenty years later, invited to write about Derrida and feminism, my subject might be "Derrida Today?"

This essay is, in particular, written for, to, and because of Ellen. Ellen is a "nineties feminist," a feminist of the generation that I, a seventies feminist, teach. I call her "Ellen" because that was the guise in which I encountered her the first time I found myself teaching Derrida in the nineties.

Spurs is Derrida's response to seventies feminism. As such, despite its apparent opposition to certain feminist positions, Spurs shares some presuppositions with the specific feminism it would critique, correct, and/or seduce. Like the feminism with which it was contemporary, Spurs belongs to the era of "woman."

The second sentence of Spurs/Éperons announces: "woman will be my subject/la femme sera mon sujet" (36). This is the first appearance of "woman" in Spurs, but it is not the first instance of the word "femme" in Éperons. The exergue contains the word "femme" but not "woman." Where the French version of the letter tells of the upcoming visit of "Wagner et sa femme," Barbara Harlow's English translation announces the visit of "Wagner and wife." In French, unlike English (but not unlike some other languages), the generic word to refer to an adult human female also denotes a particular legal, economic, and sexual status (wife), a subset of the category "woman." Synechdochally, in French (but not just in French), the word for part of the group of women stands for the whole.

This is certainly not the "femme" who made an epoch. This exergual use of "femme" is certainly marginal to Derrida's consideration of Nietzsche and women. My insistent use of "certainly" is, of course, ironic: meant to wink at Ellen, who knows that Derrida has deconstructed precisely that move which would cordon off the margins, keeping the center simple and pure, who knows that Derrida generally directs us to look seriously at such textual marginalia as exergues. But that is not all.

The inseparability of wife from woman in Spurs's inscription of "la femme" might be connected to the figure of the hymen which appears there and elsewhere in Derrida's work. Or we might remark the possessive adjective in the phrase "Wagner et sa femme." The possibility of a man's possessing a woman recalls not only Nietzsche's pronouncements—"Woman wants to be taken and accepted as a possession"[2]—but also *Spurs*'s consideration of "propriation" as central to thinking about women.

Derrida's quotation of the French translation of Nietzsche's 1872 letter draws particular attention to the phrase "Wagner et sa femme" by preceding it with the German original—"Wagner mit Frau." *Éperons* frequently supplements the French translation of Nietzsche with the original German. The exergue alone does this nine times. But—while the other eight German phrases are in either parentheses or brackets following the French text—"Wagner mit Frau" not only precedes the French but is laid out as if part of the French text, set off only in commas. Like the French "femme," the German "Frau" can mean either wife or woman. In Richard Schwaderer's German translation, *Sporen*, Derrida writes: "Die 'Frau'—das Wort macht Epoche" (49).

Ellen, a U.S. graduate student enamored of "theory," reads French and German. "Ellen" reads like a bad bilingual pun: the French female pronoun ("elle") pluralized in German ("en"). "Ellen will be my subject," I might say, translating *Spurs* in the nineties. Where, a generation ago, Derrida put "woman," I might replace the noun with a female bilingual plural pronoun. Bilingual: a word not quite in any language but marking the junctures and disjunctures between them, thus making language knotty and thick, blocking the view. A pronoun: marking the inadequacy or excessiveness of any name while standing in the place that demands a noun. Not a name and not in any mother tongue, yet despite and because, still female and plural: the subject of nineties feminism, as dreamt in *Spurs*.

If the epoch-making word in 1972 was "woman," by 1982 it was "women," emphasis on the plural. Seventies feminism envisioned a singular unity which could be collectivized under the name of woman. Woman in *Spurs* is figured as insistently plural. Derrida, through Nietzsche, criticizes feminism's desire for a singular concept of woman. Through the eighties, the feminist response to *Spurs* either used Derrida to criticize a restrictive and too singular conception of woman or criticized Derrida for speaking only of woman and not caring about women—or, and often, both.

Spurs works to make sure that Nietzsche's figuration of woman is not seen as singular. The text centers upon a numbered list of three different positions for women in Nietzsche.[3] This is probably the most often cited part of *Spurs*, the numbered paragraphs functioning as a mnemonic device, a ready-made format for note taking. The typology is, to be sure, hedged around with recognitions that it is reductive, but although three may not be enough, it will at least ward off the collapse into a single conception of woman. Yet the same word names these different positions: all three are called "woman," or taken in their plural, they are all "women."

In French: "1. La femme . . . comme figure . . . de mensonge. . . . 2. La femme . . . comme figure . . . de verité. . . . 3. La femme . . . comme puissance affirmative" [as figure of falsehood, as figure of truth, as affirmative power]. In the German translation: "1. Die Frau . . . als Bild . . . der Luge. . . . 2. Die Frau . . . als Bild . . . der Wahrheit. . . . 3. Die Frau . . . als affirmative . . . Macht." When Derrida's reading of Nietzsche is translated into German, Nietzsche's various statements about women are all grouped under the word "Frau." Even though the statements do not all use that noun.

At least two readers of *Spurs* have had occasion to comment on the German word "Frau," placing it in diacritical distinction not to a word for man, but to another word for woman. In his 1980 reading of the four-language edition of *Éperons*, Alexander Argyros interrupts his quoting of an English translation of Nietzsche after the word "women" and inserts (in brackets): "[actually 'ladies'—*frauen*, not *weiben*]."[4] Reading Derrida on Nietzsche and women, Argyros is distracted by something not in the text, by the thought of "weiben." Like "ellen," "weiben" is not a German word, but a pseudo-German plural. Sensitive to a distinction in German, Argyros feels a need for a similar distinction in English. "Frauen" is not an exact equivalent of the English "ladies"—the translator is not incorrect in using "women"—but like Argyros we might want to remember the "ladies" (as earlier we recalled the "wife") and interrupt the too smooth progress, whether in translation or otherwise, to the word "women."

"Ladies" don't appear in *Spurs*, except one. The English translation states: "In its maneuvers distance strips the lady of her identity and unseats the philosopher-knight" (53). "Lady" here translates the French "femme," where the German translation puts "Frau." Called by the proximity of "knight," the "lady" reminds us that the best equivalent of "femme" may not always be "woman." The identity the lady here loses is, in Derrida's French, "l'identité propre de la femme." The lady's rare appearance is, appropriately, on the side of the "proper." If one of the figures of woman in *Spurs* would be proper, might we not be tempted to call her a "lady"?

A few years after Argyros, another reader of *Spurs* paused over the German word for "women." At the beginning of her account of Derrida's paper, Alice Jardine supplies Nietzsche's German "die Frauen" in a parenthesis after "women." She adds a footnote: "The alternations in Nietzsche's texts between *Frau* (which has noble, wifely connotations) and *Weib* (the 'female'—at most, a prostitute) would need to be sorted out to untangle fully 'woman' . . . in his text."[5] Responsive to the same distinction as Argyros, Jardine suggests not "ladies" for "Frauen" but "female" for "Weib." If "Frauen" can be translated by "women," we need another, lower noun for "Weib." While it is not entirely correct to say that "Weib" is "at most, a prostitute," Jardine, groping like Argyros for a way to express the hierarchy in the "Frau/Weib" distinction, recalls the classic polarization of women into either wives or prostitutes.[6] Although they do not exactly succeed in mapping the German words onto the available English vocabulary, these two eighties commentaries recognize in the "Frau/Weib" distinction something which also functions in English: a hierarchy dividing and classing "women" according to an inextricable combination of sexual and economic position.

Both Argyros and Jardine slip in their attempts to translate the "Frau/Weib" distinction. It is no wonder. What is to their credit is that they notice it at all. Excellent readers of Derrida's French, Argyros and Jardine encounter Nietzsche's German in Derrida's text. Derrida, himself an excellent reader of Nietzsche's German, gives his readers no help with this aspect of the German text. Argyros and Jardine (like the present author), trained in French, barely know German. But they notice what Derrida ignores.

Some of the quotations from Nietzsche in *Spurs* use the word

"Frau"; others use the word "Weib." Sometimes these German words are even inserted parenthetically into the French or English quotations in the text. But nowhere in *Spurs* does Derrida comment upon these words. Derrida often comments not only upon Nietzsche's vocabulary, but even on his punctuation (for example: "once again the play here of both the quotation marks and the hyphens should be noted" [69]). The entire texture of *Spurs* teaches us to attend to the specificity of Nietzsche's text, rather than reduce it to its conceptual positions. But with all the attention to the fine points of Nietzsche's writing, nowhere in this essay on Nietzsche's women does Derrida remark on what even those of us who barely know German nonetheless can see from the quotations in his text: that Nietzsche sometimes speaks of "Frauen," sometimes of "Weiber."

Argyros and Jardine trip over the German terminology and then let it slide. Both notice the "Frau/Weib" distinction parenthetically, but their brilliant and careful readings of *Spurs* do not comment further upon it. Nor would I have, a decade ago. Nor could I until faced with Ellen.

The same "female" Jardine suggests as a translation for "Weib" makes a significant appearance in *Spurs*. Discussing "The History of an Error" (*The Twilight of the Idols*), Derrida writes: "In each of its . . . epochs . . . there are certain words underlined. And in the second epoch, Nietzsche has underlined only the words *sie wird Weib, elle* [*l'Idée*] *devient femme.*" Harlow translates Derrida's last phrase, his translation of "sie wird Weib," as "it becomes female."[7] In this instance where "femme" clearly translates "Weib," Harlow chooses to translate "femme" by "female" rather than "woman." For the next few pages the English refers to the "becoming-female" of the Idea when the French has "devenir-femme." Schwaderer's German translation, which generally translates Derrida's "femme" by "Frau," gives us "Weib-werden" for this phrase (69ff).

Immediately following this appearance of the "female" in *Spurs*, we read: "Heidegger cites this sequence, even respects its underlining, but . . . he skirts the woman . . . all the elements of the text are analyzed, without exception, except the idea's becoming-female (*sie wird Weib*). In such a way does one permit oneself to see without reading, to read without seeing. But if we ourselves should take a closer look at this '*sie wird Weib*' we would not be proceeding in a way *counter to* Heidegger's (such a counter direction is in fact his own)." As a reader of Nietzsche, Derrida places himself in the tradition of Heidegger which prides itself on "analyzing all the elements of the text." Derrida points out that Heidegger neglects the woman and, no less in Heideggerean tradition, Derrida skips the "Weib"—so I point out, carrying on.

I want to read the "wife," the "lady," and the "female" in *Spurs*. Yet they appear, not in Derrida's (French) text, but in its English translation. Focusing on the four-language edition of *Éperons* whose format foregrounds translation, Argyros writes: "Derrida's work clearly seeks to trouble the various 'centrisms' at work in any glib notion of translation. . . . Derrida *is* his prolongation, in stylistic mimicry or in translation" (27–28). It may be that the work of translation, the necessity of thinking on the level of word choice, carries Derrida's "femme" into a more finely articulated space—more divided and pluralized—than is possible in an all too familiar language.

And of course Derrida's French text was always already in translation—not just in the general or banal Derridean sense that every text is, but specifically in its many quotations, which are translations of Nietzsche's German. And although we cannot pick up a "wife" or a "lady" in the French, we can encounter a "female" there, precisely at a moment when Derrida pauses over Nietzsche's word choice. Quoting the translation of *Ecce Homo* where Nietzsche claims that he "connaît bien les femmes," immediately after the word "femmes," Derrida writes (in brackets): "[ou plutôt la femelle, *Weiblein*]" (104). The English translation closely renders the bracketed remark as "[or rather, the female, *Weiblein*]." Here Harlow's "female" translates not "femme" but "femelle," an actual cognate of "female." Although Nietzsche's alternation between "Frau" and "Weib" never causes Derrida to hesitate over the use of "femme," here—registering that Nietzsche is using another word for women—he is prompted, in a gesture reminiscent of Argyros, parenthetically to correct the translation.

And like Argyros, Derrida here trips a bit over the plural, correcting the translation's plural "femmes" with the singular "femelle." Nietzsche's German reads "die Weiblein," the definite article marking as plural a word ("das Weiblein") which is otherwise unchanged in the plural. As Derrida's "Weiblein" recalls Argyros's "weiben," I begin perversely to imagine the power of the grammatically incorrect plural to express something not yet fully contained and domesticated in the correct, singular woman. From wom*en* to weib*en* to ell*en*: "Ellen will be my subject"—here where "ellen" is a bad plural of "elle," as we are trying to read between three languages.

If "Weib" is lower than "Frau"—in the entangled terms of class position and sexual propriety—"Weiblein," the diminutive of "Weib," is more insistently low: dismissive, derogatory, condescending. Derrida feels it necessary to mark that lowness with "femelle," the diminutive of "femme," a word which itself is, according to my French dictionary, both pejorative and low class in usage.

"Frau/Weib/Weiblein": we have here not a binary opposition, but an active and fluid lexical distinguishing between "women" which is not at all restricted, even just in the quotations from Nietzsche in *Spurs,* to these three terms. At stake in such lexical distinctions, which can also be found—albeit differently skewed—in English and French (among other languages) are always intermingled connotations of class and sexuality. As Derrida dreams of "sexual difference," which would not be contained within a binary opposition, of "sexual differences," which would not be singular, his text trips over, catches in passing only to quickly forget other "sexual differences." These sexual differences, which cannot be called gender, construct "women" in diacritical distinction not to the opposite sex but to another class or sexuality or age. Because differences "between women" have been sexualized, no less than the difference between the sexes, distinctions of class or age operate as sexual difference.

Ellen recognizes these categories as among those which nineties feminism insists we do not collapse back into a model in which gender is the only difference that matters. "Ell/en" recognizes that as we cross between languages we run into those differences. "Women" here always designates not just gender, but also class and sexuality and age.

I added the category of "age" to my list because of the German word "Frauenzimmer," which, although it can have sexual or class connotations, always implies youth.[8] If Nietzsche's "Weiblein" causes Derrida briefly to hesitate in his use of "women," Nietzsche's "Frauenzimmer" truly gives him pause. Quoting the opening of *Beyond Good and Evil*—"Supposing truth to be a woman"—*Spurs* comes to Nietzsche's question of whether philosophers' clumsy ways of approaching truth are not inept means "pour prendre une fille" (54). Derrida inserts a parenthesis after the word "fille"— "(*Frauenzimmer*, terme meprisant: une fille facile)." The English translation of Nietzsche gives us "winning a wench" after "wench"; Derrida's parenthesis is translated by Harlow as "(*Frauenzimmer* is a term of contempt: an easy woman)." There is a line break immediately after the "Frauenzimmer" parenthesis and then we read the title of the next section.[9] After the title, the new section begins by quoting the very next sentence from *Beyond Good and Evil*; thus the section break actually interrupts the quotation. It is as if "Frauenzimmer" occasions not just a parenthesis but an actual break in the text, as if *Spurs* not only hesitates but stops short and has to start up again.

"Frauenzimmer" reappears in another parenthesis later in *Spurs*, in a quotation from *The Gay Science* which Derrida later interrupts to remind us (in brackets) to note "the play of both the quotation marks and the hyphen" (68–69). I want to pay at least as much attention to Nietzsche's slightly archaic "Frauenzimmer," here translated by "filles" in French and "women" in English. The word "Frauenzimmer" appears here in a discussion of women that begins "Endlich [finally] die Frauen:" and ends with the assertion "Das Weib ist so artistisch, Woman is so artistic," with the German included (without brackets, italics, or parentheses) in the French (and English) text. Situated between "Frauen" and "Weib," "Frauenzimmer" here marks a place in *Spurs* where the French equivalent for "women" is not "femmes" but "filles."

"Fille," the French word for daughter, is also the word for girl, "a child or a young person of the female sex." But "fille" can also mean a "young woman (femme) who leads a debauched life (especially, a prostitute)." In fact, the word "fille," used without any qualifier, implies this secondary meaning, a woman of loose morals. In order to refer to a proper young female, in French one must use the pleonasm "jeune fille" (literally, "young young person of the female sex") so as to avoid the sexuality suggested by an unaccompanied "fille." Between the age definition and the sexual definition, my French dictionary tells me that, in a usage either archaic or rustic, "fille" means "an unmarried [female] person (as opposed to 'femme')." Under this definition, we find that the somewhat oxymoronic term "fille-mère" (literally, "daughter-mother") means an unwed mother and the common but no less oxymoronic "vieille fille" (literally, "old young person of the female sex") means a likewise oxymoronic "old maid."

This dictionary (*Le Petit Robert*) likes to explain meanings through opposition or antonymy, when possible. For example, it parenthetically glosses the two primary meanings of "fille" with "as opposed to 'son' " and "as opposed to 'boy.' " With this old-fashioned or provincial sense of "fille," the dictionary uses the same antonymous formulation: "as opposed to 'femme.' " The distinction "femme/fille," presented most directly in this usage, suggests that to become a woman, one must marry; otherwise one remains in a minoritized and/or improper state. In this usage—but I would argue also implicitly in its other senses—a "fille" is *elle*-who-is-not-*femme*. And, I would further argue, that difference, the distinction femme/fille, is—no less than the opposition daughter/son or girl/boy—a sexual difference.

Nietzsche's "Frauenzimmer" brings Derrida to the "femme/fille" distinction. Its first appearance, in the quotation from *Beyond Good and Evil*, introduces the "fille" into *Spurs*. Immediately thereupon, Derrida breaks the text, ending a section. Or we might say (picking up *Spurs*'s nautical motif) that, unable to continue in the path of the "fille," Derrida comes about ("virer": changes tack, veers, turns around). When the next section begins (under a new heading), the same passage from *Beyond Good and Evil* continues. But first Derrida states: "At this moment, the truth of woman (*femme*) . . . Nietzsche turns it about (*virer*)" (54–55). Derrida's comment ends with a colon, following which the quotation from Nietzsche continues.

By thus breaking up the quotation, making it span two sections of the text, and reintroducing it with this short commentary, *Spurs* turns from the "fille" and returns to the "femme." When the quotation continues with "certainly she has not let herself be won," Nietzsche repeats the verb from the preceding sentence (German "einnehmen," French "prendre"), but, as framed in *Spurs*, "she" seems to refer to the "femme" of Derrida's introductory phrase and not the "fille" who ends the previous section ("prendre une fille"), the "Frauenzimmer" of Nietzsche's preceding sentence. Derrida immediately follows the quotation with the assertion, "la femme ne se laisse pas prendre" (does not let herself be won), reinforcing the sense that the creature who resists capture is called "femme," although in fact the verb "prendre" refers back to the phrase which ends the preceding section: "prendre une fille."[10]

Derrida's celebration of the woman who cannot be taken is, to be sure, an affirmation of what slips away from our inept attempts to pin her down and name her. Ironically, at this moment, the "fille" he encountered for the first time slips away, leaving him with the same old "femme." Ironically, the "fille" who got away is, by the philosopher's own account, "easy": "easy," implying one who can be taken. But "easy" may also imply a female who, unlike the wife, does not have a good name, is not possessed under a man's name. As the Nietzsche quotation passes from one section of the text to another where it literally appears *under* another name (under the title of the new section, "Truths"), the "fille" becomes a "femme," a passage which normatively entails a change of name.

Spurs goes on to assert: "That which . . . does not let itself be taken [prendre] is—*feminine,* which should not, however, be hastily translated by feminini*ty*, by woman's feminini*ty*, by feminine sexuali*ty*, or other essentializing fetishes which are just what one thinks one is capturing [prendre] when one has not escaped the foolish-

ness of the dogmatic philosopher . . . or the inexperienced seducer"
(54–55; emphasis in original).

"That which does not let itself be taken" refers back to Nietzsche's "she has not let herself be taken," whose "she" refers back to
Nietzsche's "Frauenzimmer"—"fille," "wench," "fille facile," "easy
woman." Derrida takes Nietzsche's phrase, transforming the feminine pronoun ("sie," "elle," "she") into the neuter construction in
order to say that all we know about "that" is that it is feminine,
meaning first of all that "it" is represented by a feminine pronoun.
When Derrida says that "it" is feminine, he is saying, among other
things, that the word for truth, in German and French ("die Wahrheit," "la vérité"), is feminine. Derrida notes the word's gender and
then warns us against proceeding too quickly from that to some
more substantive femininity.

Perhaps because I am thinking about "elle," I hear Derrida warn-
ing us not to move too quickly to any noun. "Femininity" makes a
noun out of the adjective "feminine," gives it a proper name, we
might say. By underlining the endings, he lays scornful emphasis on
the nominalization of the feminine. All the "essentializing fetishes"
he lists are nouns, as if here the process of essentializing were synonymous with nominalizing, with the making of nouns from adjec-
tives and pronouns—the noun, the name, the substantive as fetish.
It would be foolish to think one could capture her with any noun;
all he can say is that there is something feminine, what we could call
"elle." This attack on essentializing feminine fetishes is certainly a
central message of *Spurs,* and the term "essentializing" is recognizable as part of a campaign against a certain seventies feminism.

"Essentializing"—the word marks an era. Ellen is an antiessen-
tialist feminist and her antiessentialism has learned from Derrida.
Facing Ellen, I'm pleased to notice that the move he warns us
against, the move from an indefinite feminine ("elle") to a name or
substantive, is here termed hasty translation. I am further amused
to note, in the bilingual edition of *Spurs,* that the English translation
puts this as "should not be hastly [*sic*] mistaken." "Mistaken" here
renders the verb "traduire," a perfectly good equivalent of the En-

glish "translate." And, as if to enact both haste and translation as mistake, a letter is left out of "hastily."

The pauses to consider the difference between "Frau" and "Weib" or "femme" and "fille" (often marked by a bracketed intervention in a translation) could be considered defenses against what Derrida here calls hasty translation. And this particular quotation allows me to begin to dream of some solidarity between the suspicion of "essentializing feminine fetishes" and the insistence that we slow down for the bumps in passing from one language to another.

A hasty translation wants to take as little time as possible. If we would resist essentializing, we must take time. Commenting on *Spurs* at the beginning of the eighties, Argyros wrote that "Derrida *is* his prolongation . . . in translation." If translation is prolongation, hasty translation is mistaken. Translation extends Derrida in time. The present essay has been an attempt to translate *Spurs* into the nineties.

Translation in time, however, cannot be translation out of time. In responding to the question "Nietzsche today?" Derrida spoke in, for, and of the era that was 1972. By prolonging *Spurs* into the nineties, I am trying not so much to update it as to date it. Prolonging the passage of translation, I often found reason to linger among what the dictionary calls "archaic." Nietzsche's "Frauenzimmer" was (already in the nineteenth century) old-fashioned, which is why one English translator chose to render it with "wench." (And probably why another chose the more contemporary "woman.") The dusty path of "Frauenzimmer" led to two archaic usages of "fille," one debauched and the other rustic. Momentarily excited by the debauched "fille," I found the rustic definition particularly fertile. For there—out of touch with the modern era, out of step with modern woman—was made plain the assumption that a "femme" was someone married to a man. To lean thus upon the archaic is to recognize that language exists in time, that it carries a history in it, and that in it we can read traces not just of its history but of history.

The refrain of antiessentialism has moved feminism to a slow dance with history. Where in the seventies we hastily scanned history for "woman," filtering out local differences, now we try to attend precisely to those local differences, describing the varying situations of women in place and time. Nineties feminism is the context in which we must see that "women" (or some close equivalent of that word in other languages) is defined differently at different moments of the language. Vocabulary carries traces of how actual living females were defined, constrained, considered, and treated. For example, historians of the British Victorian period have called our attention to the sexualized class identities marked by words like "lady" and "female," so that we cannot blithely speak of "women" in that period as if there were any group defined solely by gender. Not to deny differences between the English and the German in the late nineteenth century, still, one might assume similar assumptions are operative in Nietzsche's context. Although I do not have the knowledge of German language and history to pursue the connotations of Nietzsche's various terms for "women," I hoped here to open up the possibility of reading his vocabulary not only as the creative choices of a singular genius but also, because it is language, as necessarily part of a sociolect, inflected by communal understandings which he might take for granted, but which become visible through passage to another language or another time.

In our U.S. context, feminists have learned not only that race was intrinsic to the definition of a "lady" in the nineteenth century but, perhaps more painfully, that it functioned likewise to define the "woman" who was liberating herself in the 1970s.[11] The latter is part of the recognition that seventies feminism was functioning in history, that we not only envisioned a future but also spoke in archaicisms. The critique of our "essentializing fetishes" has led us to historicize but has not made us less anxious about our own inevitable embedding in history. Not only is "woman" not a timeless universal, but neither are feminists: we cannot be endlessly up-to-date.

Facing Ellen, I recognize that I teach in time. How do we transmit our learning in history? When we recognize that knowledge is not timeless and unchanging? In the seventies my feminist certainties were shook up by something I would call learning in an encounter with something we might call Derrida. I fantasize that Derrida might have had similar encounters with what he calls Nietzsche.

And that would be why he would want to transport Nietzsche into 1972, into dialogue with seventies feminism. Most of what I have to teach I might have learned from Derrida, whom I read for the first time in 1972. If I would teach what as a seventies feminist I learned from *Spurs*, I must *for the moment* transmit it in the nineties.

In 1992 I saw Ellen while I read *Spurs*. Ellen prized *Spurs* for the way it put seventies feminism in its place. I wanted to "show her," by putting *Spurs* in its place, showing how behind it was from the point of view of nineties feminism. Derrida seemed suddenly out of it, stuck on a single, binary notion of sexual difference when we could see multiple sexual differences all around. Did I make Derrida look old-fashioned in order to appear up-to-date myself?

Spurs today? Derrida's timely intervention called into question a certain essentializing of woman in seventies feminism. No longer in that era, we can see that, however much it questioned seventies "woman," *Spurs* was not beyond what it questioned, but was in engagement with it, sharing the assumption that, in thinking about women, what we since have called gender, was the only pertinent category and that the only difference that was sexual was the distinction male/female.

This dates *Spurs*. To read Derrida as if he were writing outside of history would not only put him in the position of timeless master, but also and in the same gesture render him obsolete. Derrida took pains to date his text and I want to read rather than erase those marks. He wrote in, for, and of the era marked by the word "woman," and I want to read that word as the mark of an era.

Eight Castration Anxiety and the Unemployed Ph.D.

Twenty-three years ago was my first year on the job market; I went to the 1975 MLA convention in San Francisco. My boyfriend Alex was on the market too; we had booked a room at the cheapest convention hotel and gotten a good deal on our flights. And then, a week before the MLA, the airline we were flying went on strike. So Alex and I took the Greyhound bus from Ithaca, New York, to San Francisco and back.

Half my life ago, I remember that journey as a "great adventure," the only time I crossed the country by land. I remember crossing the expanse of Nebraska on Christmas Day, feeling fortunate because Christmas pretty much emptied out the bus, affording us the Greyhound riders' most coveted luxury—each of us had a double seat to ourselves. We had quickly learned the veteran rider's trick of positioning ourselves in the aisle seat and appearing to be asleep whenever the bus came to a station: no one with another choice will wake someone, and so we guarded our double seats against those we had come to see as neophytes and interlopers, those riding for only a couple hundred miles.

We didn't fare nearly as well at the MLA. While Alex and I had four interviews each, neither of us got an on-campus "call-back."

Late in the spring both of us did manage to land temporary leave-replacement jobs. Alex was the luckier—he got a one-year full-time position. I ended up with a one-semester stint teaching three courses for a total of $3,900.

At the end of that semester I returned to Ithaca, an unemployed Ph.D. Thanks to a rent-free extra bedroom in the apartment of a guy who owed Alex money, I was able to live for a few months on what I had managed to save from my $3,900. Thus free all day, I felt I should try to turn my dissertation into a book, but found I was unable to work. Weeks and months went by, during which I did nothing—I guess I must have been depressed. Sometimes I would go to the university, to the department where I'd been a graduate student; my teachers seemed embarrassed to see me. I felt they were rejecting me because I was a failure; it was only years later (when I had unemployed dissertators of my own) that I understood that my teachers couldn't bear to see me because it made them feel guilty.

The one thing I did do during that period was go to bars and pick up men. Or rather, it would be more precise to say I let them pick me up: I would dress up, go to a bar, and go home with whoever asked me.

I was lucky. By April of that unemployed semester I learned that I would have a tenure-track job the next fall. Since then I've never again been unemployed and never again felt compelled to visit a bar and go home with whoever would have me. At the time, I thought of my bar excursions as sexual adventure, amusing diversion from the dreariness of my life. But years later, securely tenured, I thought back to that time, and I realized that my bar behavior had everything to do with my experience of the job market.

I went to the bar as if to the MLA, dressed to look as good as possible, ready to chat responsively (attentively, cleverly) with whoever chose to talk to me. I would always go alone and sit at the bar between two empty stools so as to signal my availability. Above all, I was enacting my passivity, my sense of having no choice, of taking whatever I could get. I was prepared (eager even) to go with *whoever* wanted me. Night after night at the bar I got what I couldn't in the profession: there was always someone who wanted me.

I felt rejected by the profession, undesired and undesirable. I was consoling myself in the bar, proving over and over that I was in fact desirable. But there is more: I was taking the painful experience of powerlessness, passivity, and lack of choice forced upon me by the profession and reenacting it as a sexual scene. I thus gave myself a sense of choosing, of *choosing not to choose*, of choosing passivity. That sense of choosing transformed the situation, made it adventurous and sexy; it gave me a sense of agency.

I do not at all regret this acting out. I tell it here not as a cautionary tale but as an example. Not that I'm proposing sex with strangers as the solution to the jobseeker's dilemma. But jobseeking is not just a socioeconomic situation; it is also a resonant psychological scenario.

What discourse we as a profession have produced around "the job market" has tended to be socioeconomic—not the sort of discourse we in the MLA are either particularly good at or particularly responsive to. Although as a profession we certainly need the socioeconomic analyses, they are of limited benefit to the individual jobseeker in coping with her situation.

In 1998, twenty-three years later, I returned to San Francisco, this time to give a paper at the MLA convention in a forum entitled "Tales from the Job Front." I took the direction of that forum to mark a shift from these quantitative social scientific analyses to a different mode of knowledge. The panel title replaces the socioeconomic connotations of "the market" with the personal adventure and traumatic-stress psychology of "the front" and, by focusing on "tales," on the story, moves to terrain more familiar to us literary scholars. In keeping with this general direction of that forum, I told a "tale" that includes sex so as to move our analysis of life on the job front not only to psychology but to psychoanalysis.

"Psychoanalysis"—that much debated practice—can mean, I know, many things to many people. I am using it here as a shorthand for a discourse spoken at the MLA, a theoretical approach used for interpreting cultural texts. The story I told suggests a psychoanalytic approach, first of all because of its focus on the sexual, but also because of its emphasis on subjectivity. It is not just a tale of powerlessness, but an example of someone grappling with powerlessness. The point of the story is that an event does not simply happen to a person but is something a person responds to and makes meaning of. I offer it as a case study in what a victim of social forces will do in order to hold onto a sense of her own agency.

Within the socioeconomic discourses typically applied to the job situation, the individual jobseeker cannot help but seem a passive victim buffeted about by the winds of the market. Although motivated by the most sympathetic intentions, such objectifying analyses may in fact add to the jobseeker's demoralizing sense of powerlessness.

I believe a psychoanalytic perspective could actually address rather than simply reinforce this sense of powerlessness. Psychoanalysis has, to be sure, all too often been used in a reductive, objectifying way, taking the individual's experience as merely an instance of the prefabricated, generic story. Nevertheless, I propose we approach the jobseeker's situation from the perspective of psychoanalysis, as the responsive practice it can be, it ought to be. The "psychoanalytic" approach I am proposing is a perspective which takes each individual, no matter how unfortunate, to be the subject of her own life story. For, if there is anything that might be in even *scarcer* supply in this market than jobs, it is the jobseeker's sense of agency, the sense precisely of being the subject of one's own life story.

■   ■   ■

Five years ago, I was standing in a locker room with my clothes off. A few lockers away, likewise undressed, stood a woman I knew socially, a woman I knew to be on the academic job market for a second year, having turned up nothing her first year. I asked how her job search was going. In the course of the conversation, I revealed that I had been an unemployed Ph.D. "Really?" she asked, clearly incredulous. My revelation appeared to relax her, to loosen her tongue. Whereas her earlier responses to my inquiry sounded strained and embarrassed, she now spoke freely of her situation, asking my advice.

I would love to report that I gave her some bit of brilliant advice that got her a job. But I didn't, and in fact I have no idea what that would be. She did, however, appear to benefit from the conversation, to get from it a sense that her situation, however difficult, was not shameful, not a mark of her own personal failing.

Standing there in the locker room, both of us saw something we hadn't expected. She learned of my trouble finding a job; I learned that the fact that I had had such trouble truly surprised her and that learning about it seemed to change how she felt about her own difficulty. I have no idea whether this revelation had any lasting effect on her, but it has in fact stayed with me.

I suspect this locker room scene is the fantasy behind this essay. I want to reveal that I was an unemployed Ph.D. in the hope that my story could make a difference to those struggling to find a job. But beyond the simple disclosure, I would also like to ponder why my companion was surprised and why that surprise seemed to have a salutary effect.

The woman in the locker room was well informed: she was familiar with the statistics about the job market; she had the information necessary to conclude that her difficulty was a common condition, not a personal failing. But whereas the statistics did not keep her from blaming herself, it seemed like my story could, at least momentarily.

To be crudely, nakedly psychoanalytic: she had presumed that I was phallic and she was castrated. There in the locker room, I revealed my castration to her, and it seemed to have the effect of diminishing her anxiety and her shame.

■   ■   ■

Castration anxiety on the job market—that's my point here. Before I move to my conclusion, one more little tale from the job front:

In response to the tight situation of the mid-nineties, a Ph.D.-granting English department held a workshop for its graduate students on the market. A tenured faculty member suggested that on December 15 job seekers should phone any schools where they had applied from which they had not yet heard. As she put it: "You don't want to sit by the phone like a girl waiting for a date."

Let me say first of all that I think this is bad advice. While I well understand how intolerable that waiting, that sense of powerlessness, can be, I personally think you'd be better off going to a bar and picking up strangers.

Although I am wary of passing along this bad advice, I have nonetheless decided to include it here on account of the little "story" that accompanied the advice. The story was originally used as a cautionary tale: "you don't want to find yourself in this position; don't let this happen to you!" I, however, am retelling it not as a cautionary tale but as an example. I want it to exemplify the connection between anxiety about the job market and "castration."

I'm using "castration" here in a loosely Lacanian tradition, where it refers to a subject's finding himself inscribed in a symbolic order he does not control. Although inscription in such a symbolic order is in fact the lot of any and every subject, most of the time we are happily unaware of it. "Being on the market," however, positions a subject so that he is likely to become all too aware, painfully aware, of his subjection to something like the symbolic order. Because "the job market" operates like an image of the symbolic order, those subjected to it, those who have put themselves on the market, are likely to confront an image of their "castration."

While I find this abstract Lacanian understanding of castration very useful in thinking about the job market, as a feminist I want to underline the fact that "castration" is also about gender. And it is as a feminist that I value this anecdote of bad professional advice—because it reveals the gendered anxiety that haunts the job front. The tenured professor's cautionary tale reminds me that castration anxiety is, after all, the fear of becoming a girl. The fear of becoming precisely the kind of girl who waits by the phone—passively sexual, sexually passive.

I believe that the jobseeker's objectively difficult situation is considerably exacerbated by just such sexual and gendered anxieties. (And the fact that the remark is made by a tenured woman can serve to remind us that it isn't just men who fear being relegated to girl status.) My hope would be that, as feminists, we might discover alternatives to shame and anxiety when we find ourselves feeling like a girl.

■   ■   ■

"Castration": the word itself grates. Combining both a threat to masculinity and a sexist perspective demeaning to women, the term is able to offend the most masculinist men and the most feminist women. I suppose that is, in part, why I like it.

The word "castration" can represent what people don't like about psychoanalysis and at the same time it can conjure up what people fear about feminism. To those of us in the MLA, however, the term has lost its bite. We're inured to the discourse of psychoanalysis and the discourse of feminism; we in the MLA are even used to the discourse of psychoanalytic feminism. "Castration" has appeared dozens of times in the MLA convention program.

Yet I had, I will admit, a certain frisson of transgression when I placed it in the title of my 1998 MLA talk. The two terms of my title—"castration anxiety" and "the unemployed Ph.D."—are, to say the least, an odd couple. Whether the juxtaposition of the two terms strikes one as comic or offensive, my title produces its effect by coupling terms belonging to two different discourses.

The funny thing is that these two discourses go about their parallel, nonintersecting business side by side at the MLA convention every year. Both phrases in my title are likely to be found in the MLA program, but they have always been segregated into separate sessions. There are the sessions where we present and discuss our scholarship, and then there are the other sort of sessions where we orient the jobseeker or discuss the plight of the profession.

When I composed my title, I wanted to cross the discursive line between the two MLAs. I am a psychoanalytic feminist theorist, and when I was asked to speak about the job market, I felt it crucial that I speak in the language of my discipline, in the language that represents my most rigorous intellectual work.

We have responded to the crisis in our profession by "getting serious," which all too often seems to mean relinquishing the thinking that we do best, the sort of thinking represented by our scholarship. Thus we end up subscribing to the general prejudice that our scholarship is abstruse, impractical, a luxury—a prejudice against academia and the humanities not unconnected to the decline in tenure-track jobs that is the source of our current job crisis.

All too often in the face of a crisis, we have acted as if the knowledge we hold so dear, the knowledge we devote our lives to, is of no practical value to us. Rather than always turning to outside experts for help with our problems, experts from positivistic disciplines that many of us have devoted decades to critiquing, we need to give it our best thought. We need to cross the line between the two MLAS, to connect our scholarship with our professional situation. We need to try to think professionally about the profession.

The paper you are about to read was presented at the English Institute, in Cambridge, Massachusetts, on October 3, 1999. I tell you
this at the outset because the paper still bears the marks of the
occasion for which it was written. While it did begin as a piece of
writing, it was not written for the temporally diffuse audience of
publication.

You reading this now are not quite the "you" the text addresses.
But, in that, you are in fact not so different from the original audience in Cambridge that Sunday morning. Although the English
Institute was where this paper first saw the light of day, the talk was
not written for that occasion either; my reading it there was a dress
rehearsal. The real event, the event that caused this piece of writing,
came later, six days later, in Minnesota.

The temporality of writing is, to be sure, incurably odd. You are
reading this in some present moment which I, in what is now for me
the present of writing, can only imagine, anticipate, and pretend to
join you in with my direct address, my present tense verbs and
second person pronouns, as if we were talking, as if we were in some
here and now together. While writing is in this way generally off-
kilter and belated, this paper will make you specifically aware of an

event you missed (unless you happen to be one of the three hundred people who were present in Minnesota on that Saturday evening). Not the moment of writing, which is nearly always an event missed by the reader, but the moment for which the paper was written.

The paper is very much about how reading and writing might allow us to connect across distance, to bond in some mediated way rather than in the romantic immediacy of the here and now, to connect across time and space rather than in the intimacy of presence. Thus can I hope that the awkward framing, the various times and spaces of my writing and its audiences, will successfully "forward" the paper and its effects to you. (When you reach the end of the paper, you will know why I put "forward" in quotation marks, what I am referring to here, in anticipation of your reading and in retrospection of my writing.)

■　■　■

This paper is written to be presented next Saturday at a conference on feminism and rhetoric at the University of Minnesota. Without that event, at that place and time, the paper would never have been written, never even have been conceived. The paper is so dependent upon that event that I was not able to produce a version of it for you that sublimates the context.

A year and a half ago when I received the invitation to speak at the conference in Minnesota, I read the date—October 9, 1999—and immediately thought "that's my sister's fiftieth birthday!" Because my sister lives in Minnesota, I fantasized giving a talk in honor of her on her birthday with her in the audience. So "sisterhood" in my title is first of all not figurative sisterhood, that is, feminism, but literal sisterhood. This paper is about my relation to my sister.

Because it is written as a sort of present to my sister, I had to package it for the moment I will give it to her. I had to put her first, before you, my esteemed colleagues at the English Institute. So I wrote it very much imagining her there. The paper begins like this: "Today, October ninth, 1999, is my sister's fiftieth birthday. Judi lives in St. Paul and is here with us this evening. This paper is dedicated to her: Happy Birthday, Judi."

Although I felt I must put Judi first, I hope of course that the paper will be of value to a more general audience. The paper in fact explicitly treats the problem of my double address (to my sister *and* to my academic colleagues), but my double address is for me most anxiously embodied by the double scene of my delivering this paper. A scene in which the "original" moment, the one for which it is written, comes second.

Aside from my hope that the paper will have value beyond its occasion, I take solace in the fact that our topic here at the English Institute is in fact "Literature, Anxiety, Temporality." I do in fact literally feel anxious about the relation between my writing and temporality as I sit here before you this morning. I can at least hope that you will see the odd "present" of my paper as, if not a theorization of anxiety and temporality, at least a telling case.

The possibility of my being "a case" reminds me of an old joke, a favorite in my family, to which my sister has alluded several times in the last couple weeks. The joke runs: "My sister is at Harvard.—Oh, what's she studying?—She's not studying anything; they're studying her." Although I sort of enjoy becoming an old family joke about academia, I also hope we can take the strange absent present of my paper, its anticipatory temporality, as matter for our discussion of the present, and especially of that strange present which is the present of writing.

In any case, my apologies for not being completely here.

■ ■ ■

When I received my invitation to speak in Minnesota, I began to fantasize dedicating my talk to Judi, as a sort of birthday toast. The more I thought about it, the more intricate the fantasy became, the more seriously my thought of Judi became intricated with the conference topic. I want to do more than just dedicate this paper to Judi; I want the dedication to my sister to be more than an extrinsic gesture; I want the dedication to be inseparable from the main point of the paper. This paper is about my relation to my sister, about the rhetoric of my relation to my sister, and, by focusing on the specific case of my relation to Judi, it is an attempt to think through a major rhetorical problem of feminism—a problem we might call "sisterhood."

My topic here arose, thus, coincidentally. I wouldn't have thought to write this paper if not for the temporal and spatial coincidence of an invitation to speak in the Twin Cities on this particular date. I stress the "occasional" nature of my talk, not however for you to dismiss it as minor, as tangential embellishment, but because I believe in the fertility of the specific as the site of productive thinking. This foregrounding of my talk's "occasional" status has everything to do with the question of rhetoric. Dedications and occasional pieces are classic rhetorical stock; they are rhetorical sites where discourse is knotted to the extradiscursive, to the here and now, to real life. Call me a deconstructionist if you like, but personally I don't take rhetorical gestures as frosting spread on top of thought; I take rhetoric to be the very place where thought happens. I don't want the dedication to be a mere flourish laid "on top of" the real paper; I want the address to my sister to be central to the paper—essential, intrinsic.

My rhetorical situation in this paper is complicated—actually, is fraught—because of the peculiarity of my address. I am speaking at an academic conference as a feminist theorist *about* my relation to my sister; I am also speaking *to* my sister, my sister who is neither an academic nor a feminist. That double address seems a tightrope walk without a net. If I speak simply as an academic theorist *about* my sister, not only will I be using her, exploiting her, alienating her, but I will be doing so in her presence and will thus have to answer to her. If, on the other hand, I speak simply *to* Judi, staying within the terms of her and my conversation, I will exclude the rest of the audience and fail to produce the more generally applicable knowledge that would justify my taking your time and attention here.

Although I don't think I can mend this divide, can't pull this odd double address together and unify what I have to say, I would like at least to put it on the agenda, to bear it in mind. I need to keep both my audiences in mind, both you, my academic feminist colleagues, and you, my only sister. It is, I think, precisely that awkward double address which I would call the rhetoric of sisterhood, the uncomfortable, fraught rhetorical situation feminists must negotiate when we speak *about and to* other women, women who don't already participate in our discourse.

Sisterhood is not a tangential rhetorical problem for feminism; it is one of feminism's central rhetorical problems. Thirty years ago, in the first flush of "women's liberation," when the second wave was just cresting, "sisterhood" was pretty much a synonym for "feminism." Cozier, less philosophical, it connoted not so much the long history of women's bondage, but a more optimistic emphasis on women bonding. Robin Morgan's 1970 anthology *Sisterhood Is Powerful* can serve as the landmark here.

Fourteen years later, Morgan published another anthology, this one called *Sisterhood Is Global.* The title's "Global" betokens the hard lesson U.S. feminism was by then trying to learn about our own ethnocentrism; the title's "Sisterhood" is an attempt to stretch that all too domestic term to incorporate feminism's new range. It is indeed, as we say, "a stretch." The idea of "sisterhood" was in fact based upon the very same domesticating blind spots that the move toward the global attempts to get beyond. By 1984, the term "sisterhood" is an anachronism; Morgan's attempt to update it is an embarrassment.

I know it's tacky to say "I told you so," but, personally, I had always found the term "sisterhood" problematic. Even in the heady days when I was a proud women's libber, I was nonplussed by the celebration of "sisterhood" around me. Not, to be sure, because I was in any way worried about ethnocentrism. Rather because "sisterhood" could not help but recall my relation to Judi, and that did not seem at all like the female bond idealized under the term; my relation to Judi did not seem at all like feminism.

What it did seem like was sibling rivalry. Judi is two and a half years older; we shared a room, sleeping in twin beds in the girlie white furniture set; I was named Jane because at the time there was a radio show called "Judy and Jane": we were meant to be a matched set. And in our slotted similarity and felt difference, we did not bond, we competed. We competed for privileges, for our mother's love and attention, for our little brother's love once he was born, and for the love and attention our father could never much afford to show us.

It is through this structure of rivalry that I understand the contrast between Judi and me. As if our rivalry meant we had to become different sorts of girls, contrasting types of girls. Since neither of us wanted to be second best, we adopted differing ideals, opposing models and goals. Competing on different terms, we might avoid definitive comparison.

When still a teenager, Judi took over the cooking in our family home; down at the University of Minnesota she majored in home economics. Cooking has always made me anxious, and I actually haven't done it at all for more than a decade. Judi said she was going to college to "get her MRS. degree"; I wanted to get a Ph.D. even though I didn't really know what it was. At the age of twenty-five, Judi had a wonderful big wedding in a beautiful white dress, preceded by a season of wedding showers—an event and a season that were the high point of her life, a dream come true. I never married. She wagered everything, bet her life, her happiness, on normative femininity; I was trying to win at a different game.

Feminism is not irrelevant to the difference between us; feminism might in fact name the difference between us. She never stopped trying to reap the benefits promised to good girls; I embraced feminism as the critique of the femininity at which I never could excel.

Within feminism, I heard rosy tales of the closeness between sisters, sisters bonding together against abusive parents, against an abusive world. But Judi and I were not close. It was not just that we were different—different interests, different values—it was that we each had a tremendous stake in our difference. Our differing choices about femininity mattered to us a lot: once they had been our strategies to compete against each other for the love we both wanted; now they were our dearest identities. It was not a matter of indifference to either of us whose choice was best.

Feminism told me that my choice was best; that Judi was wrong; that she had chosen the losing path. It was not just that Judi wasn't a feminist, that we didn't have that in common; it was that my investment in feminism was an investment in doing it better than Judi. Feminism was not a standpoint outside our sibling rivalry; it was a move within it.

And yet feminism wants to be for all women. Feminism derives its authority from the rhetorical claim to speak for the interests of women in general, rather than only for a restricted group of women, rather than only for self-identified feminists. In relation to that claim, feminism has always found the nonfeminist woman a thorny problem, a gnawing contradiction. Does feminism speak for those women who don't identify as feminists? Are they our constituency or our adversaries? If we speak for them in disregard of what they themselves would say, how then can we speak to them?

As a feminist theorist, I found myself abstractly pondering this philosophical and rhetorical knot; at the same time, though without seeing any connection, I also struggled with the ongoing personal problem of my relation to my sister. It wasn't that we had no relation whatsoever, but we had never found a relation in which we could both be comfortable.

Thirty-two years ago Judi moved from our home in Duluth down to the Twin Cities to attend the University of Minnesota; since that time we have always lived in different cities. Over those years, we have tried to connect through various media. We visited each other a couple of times, even had a few nights out drinking. (Those were the most successful, lubricated by alcohol; I discovered over a pitcher of margaritas that Judi could drink me under the table, something I admire in a woman.) There was a brief period about a dozen years ago when we spoke on the phone regularly. At the time we both had young sons and that seemed momentarily to give us a common ground. But neither the face-to-face meetings nor the phone calls ever managed to establish a relation we knew how to be in together; we kept bumping up against the awkwardness of our differences.

Two years ago, Judi and I happened upon a new medium. We started writing email to each other. Since then we've been writing regularly: Judi writes me pretty much every day; I write her a little less often, but still with a dailiness. She has become the person in my birth family to whom I am closest, the one who knows most about my present life. Judi and I now have a relation, a real live relation; we now have something I might want to call "sisterhood." And we have it on and through email. (Pretty much exclusively in fact: we have not been able to transfer this email connection either to face-to-face or even to the phone.)

The title of my paper, "Econstructing Sisterhood," refers to our email relation. The title is meant to suggest that "sisterhood" is not something given but something we build, and that I'm going to tell you the story about how the specific medium of email allowed Judi and me together to construct a bond.

Some would say that email is a paltry bond, and that the fact that we cannot transfer the connection to a more live medium cheapens it, points to its limitation. Well, I'm not denying its limitations, but I want instead to insist that the very constraints of email, its forms and modes—in short, its "rhetoric"—enabled a relation where there wasn't one before.

The idea of a "sisterhood" constructed through such highly technological means is surprising. By referring to a familial, biological or domestic, bond, "sisterhood" tends to suggest a relation that is natural, intimate, less mediated. When we use it figuratively (as in the rhetoric of feminism), it suggests something natural and cozy. And those connotations do not jibe with email—the computer, technology, writing, the disembodied connection—writing without the hand (without a signature to mark bodily presence). An econstructed sisterhood is a technologically dependent bond. And our romantic notions—which tend to be particularly strong around issues of women, family, feminism, and bonding—make us suspicious of such an obviously technologically mediated form.

The usual connotations of the term "sisterhood" clash with the connotations of "email." Worse yet, my title introduces the horrid neologism "econstructing" because in its awkwardness, unfamiliarity, and shorthand it carries a lot of the graceless, unromantic style of email. The two words in my title embody the clash between two different sets of connotations, two different rhetorics.

The two words of my title can also serve to figure the relation itself. Like those two words, Judi and I have not merged our differences into an overarching unified style. Like my title this morning, our email remains awkward but it manages to mean and to communicate.

Feminism has spent the last twenty years working on an ethics that respects the differences between women. I'm beginning to suspect that, even more than an ethics, what we need is a rhetoric. In light of that, I'd like to propose this email correspondence as a model for communicating across difference. My point is not that we should all start finding nonfeminist, nonacademic pen pals. Rather I want to present this email relation as an example of a bond that negotiates limitation.

■   ■   ■

Judi writes me pretty much every day. In fact when I'm out of town and can't check my email, she still writes me every day. She says that writing me functions like a diary and so she wants to do it daily even if I'm not reading it daily. I write a bit less often, around five times a week, but my messages are also "daily," in the sense that I generally talk about things I've done in the last day and things I will do in the next day or two, as well as some reflections on how I feel about those things.

The daily format allows us to cover a wide range of topics. Both of us write about things that happen at work, about our children, about purchases, household chores, sex, social events, bodily events (illness, weight). Although our lives are in many ways not similar, the daily format provides an organizing device that can include widely dissimilar things.

But these messages are not just a double-entry diary. Both of us respond to things the other says about her life. Not to everything, but to whatever happens to prompt response. And it is these responses that are, to my mind, the most valuable part of the email.

To convey the value of these responses, I need to contrast them with another relation, because we appreciate our email in contrast to that other relation: Judi and I enjoy how our email differs from phone conversations with our mother. We both talk regularly on the phone with Mom: Judi speaks to her at least once a day (Mom also lives in the Twin Cities now); I call her every Saturday morning. Although Judi talks to Mom a lot more often than I do, in both cases the telephone is the major mode of contact: both of us talk to her much more often than we see her. And both of us find our phone calls with Mom frustrating, in pretty much the same way.

Judi and I complain to each other that Mom doesn't listen to us. Judi and I give each other the kind of attention we find hard to get from our mother. I imagine we know how to be attentive in just the right way, because we were both schooled by our frustration with the same style of inattentiveness.

There are two different ways in which Mom doesn't listen. Sometimes she talks at length about herself and her life and literally does not listen when I try to tell her something about my life. While that is her at her worst, it is a not-uncommon telephone event, as if it were something about the phone. The other way she "doesn't listen" is that sometimes in response to things I say about my life or feelings, she jumps in too fast with ready-made advice, with solutions that are inattentive to the particular situation. In other words, sometimes she literally does not listen; other times when she hears what I say, she responds in a way that makes me feel like she isn't "really listening."

In order to appreciate my sister here, I find myself criticizing my mother. In terms of the general concept of "sisterhood," of bonds between women, that is certainly worth noting, and a complicated thing it is indeed. The complications are hardly just theoretical. My mother too will be there, sitting right next to Judi, listening to me. If this talk is a birthday gift to Judi, I fear it might be Mom who's paying for it.

On the other hand, maybe the problem is not so much Mom but rather the phone. As I said, the basic medium of my relation to Mom is the telephone, and what I prefer about my relation to Judi may well have to do with the difference between email and phone. As part of an attempt to think of an econstructed sisterhood as a relation in which the email is not extrinsic, not a mere carrier of the relation, but is in fact intrinsic, literally constitutive of the bond, I would like for a moment to focus specifically on these media, to consider why email might be better than phone as a means of communicating across difference.

Although the phone is a distance technology, it is one that feels immediate: you talk in synch time; you hear the other's voice. Perhaps most importantly, you are talking not writing. I think the main thing that allows Judi and me to be attentive to each other, to "listen" to each other, is that we are in fact not "listening," we are reading.

I always reread Judi's emails at least once before I write back. I know she prints mine out and refers to them in writing her response. This is not spontaneous communication: it is an exchange of pause, consideration, thoughtfulness; it is a technology of reading and writing. Call me a deconstructionist if you like, but personally I suspect reading and writing to be more respectful of difference than can be the illusion of immediacy we have on the phone.

Of course, there is a downside to writing—one I believe Derrida called "dissemination"—writing's propensity to stray outside the intended scene of address. Some months after Judi and I started emailing regularly, I discovered that Judi printed up my emails and gave them to Mom. I don't know if that began as a sporadic practice, but now she always passes my emails on.

This was not what I had in mind. I imagined Judi and I had a private one-on-one relation, which I valued because it was outside the family system. When I discovered that Judi put our private relation into general circulation I felt a bit betrayed; later, I decided it didn't really matter.

(As I write this, I wonder what relation there is between Judi's showing our email to Mom and my "showing" our email to all of you here. I mean *who*, after all, is "putting our private relation into general circulation"?)

I should say that Judi does not in fact circulate every word I write her. She edits my emails for Mom's eyes, taking out anything she doesn't want Mom to know, anything she thinks I wouldn't want Mom to know, and anything she thinks Mom wouldn't want to know. Although occasionally I will say "oh, I guess you'll have to edit out this paragraph," generally I submit myself to her editing without comment. Judi does not circulate the email she writes.

Although I never directly asked her, I have wondered why she would want to show Mom the emails. I have to admit that I thought about her tattling on me when we were kids, her running to Mom and getting me in trouble. Her circulating my emails has not, however, gotten me into trouble (that awaits this talk). Her showing Mom has in fact done the opposite of getting me into trouble: Mom has told me (on the phone of course) that she values my emails, not only because she learns about my life, but because from my responses she learns more about what's going on in Judi's life.

These phone conversations with Mom about my emails suggest a much more complicated circuitry than the simple opposition between phone and email, Mom and Judi, that I posited a bit ago. These two different relations not only exist in contrast with each other; they actually affect each other. I know that I have had some good phone conversations with Mom precisely because of her reading my emails to Judi.

Whatever the complications of this sister/mother circuit, Judi and I bond quite comfortably around how we feel about Mom. Dad, however, is another story. I am pretty angry at Dad, feel he was not a good father to his daughters; Judi, on the other hand, seems largely uncritical of him and generally takes his side. Ironically, I often feel my anger at Dad most sharply when I think of Judi: I tend to blame him for her difficulties, her unhappiness, her insecurity. Although my anger at Dad makes me feel close to Judi in my head, in reality, it produces distance between us: it is the thing we can least agree on, least share.

I fantasize that Judi and I could bond in our common suffering at Dad's hands. I see in her so much that resembles my own plight as a daughter wounded by her father's preference for his son. I imagine that if only Judi too could get angry at Dad then she would be happy, could claim her right to what she desires.

My anger at Dad, my sense that he's to blame for my sister's suffering, we might want to call that "feminism." I think my fantasy here is very much the feminist fantasy of "sisterhood": a fantasy of "saving" my sister by making her more like me, a fantasy rooted in my belief that she really is like me but doesn't know it.

In reality, however, Judi and I are able to keep talking, are able to bond by letting our opposed views of Dad stand, by agreeing to disagree. Ironically, in order to construct our sisterhood, I must resist my fantasy of "sisterhood." This is a "sisterhood" across rather than within feminism.

∎　∎　∎

Before concluding, I'd like to consider one more aspect of my correspondence with Judi, an aspect that may well seem trivial. For more than a year now, I have been reporting weekly to Judi on my weight. Every Monday I weigh myself at the gym and then report what I call my "official weigh-in" on email. While I actually weigh myself every day—usually several times a day on a couple of different scales— what makes this weighing "official" is only that this is the weight I report to Judi. I have taken Judi as authoritative witness in my relation to my own weight. I should specify that Judi does not in fact know what I weigh (I imagine she would be horrified to know how large the number is, and I'm certainly not going to reveal it here). I don't report my weight but rather how much I have gone up or down from the week before.

To explain the significance of this ritual gesture, I need to gloss the history of my relation to my weight. I think eating/dieting has long been a central register of the opposition between Judi and me, perhaps even *the* central register. I remember a moment from our adolescence when Judi, dieting, was prodding me to eat the chocolate chip cookies she had baked, cookies she was not eating.

The centrality of this register is no doubt attributable to its centrality in my family of origin. I think all the moral and psychological issues—questions of good and bad, of pleasure and control—are in my family most densely clustered around eating.

Judi is thin, and I'm not; this opposition is undoubtedly constructed not given. (In fact as young children, Judi was chubby and I was thin.) Judi controls her weight, does not allow herself to gain weight, eats a very low-fat diet. I, on the other hand, have resisted controlling my weight for my entire adult life, feel militant about my right to eat fat, and like to define myself as the kind of woman who does not diet, who eats as much as she wants. Embracing the right to eat fat, I have defined myself not only differently but precisely as *not* the kind of woman my sister is.

Despite this opposition, or maybe in some way because of it, a little more than a year ago I found myself wanting to deliver my relation to my weight up to Judi's gaze. I had decided I wanted to lose weight, and admitting that to myself, I went on to admit it to Judi. It seemed a step beyond opposition, a moment of admitting that I was more like her than I liked to pretend. It felt like some form of giving in, of giving up a resistance. It also felt like giving Judi the power to criticize me, the power to feel superior. I took her as witness to my attempt to do something I knew her to be better at than me. I was asking for her help.

Her response has surprised me. I thought I was giving her the power to put me down; I expected a superior, withering gaze; I found instead an unforeseen generosity. Reporting my weight to Judi has become important to me: I often rush home from the gym on Mondays to write her right away; I feel proud when I can report a loss and am always gratefully relieved when she forgives my lapses and encourages me not to give up.

Last Monday, September 27, 1999, at 6:32 P.M., I wrote Judi: "Excellent weigh-in to report today. I lost three and a half pounds since last week. Last week I was up two, but that still means a loss of a pound and a half from my low of two weeks ago. This is my last weigh-in before my trip. I'll try not to gain too much during the trip so you can be proud of how I look (course compared to you I will always look fat . . .)."

A paragraph break and then my email continues: "Wish I had as good news on my writing. I'm trying to write an ending to EcoSis. I wrote two stinking pages which I will throw away tomorrow. I felt dead in the head. I feel like I just wish it were done, but I have to have a great ending."

Judi wrote me at 7:10 P.M.: "Nice weight loss. . . . Keep it going for the next month and you could be at a ten pound loss by Halloween. [new paragraph] Hope you found an ending to me. . . . . [ellipsis Judi's]."

Then at 7:18 P.M., she sent me another email. This one was not "written to me," but was "forwarded." She had been sent it by Shawna, a woman she used to work with, a woman who used to French braid Judi's hair during breaks at work. Shawna had not written it but was likewise "forwarding" it, not just to Judi but to a whole list of people.

This forwarded email, circulating quickly between so many people—surely some of you have received it—is not only a quintessential email (by being so rapidly and widely circulated) but is in fact a meta-email. It is not just an email message but a message about emails. Its subject is: "Eleven reasons why email is like a penis."

Reason # 10: "Those who have it think that those who don't are somehow inferior." Reason # 9: "Those who don't have it may agree that it's neat, but think it's not worth the fuss that those who have it make about it." Reason # 6: "In the distant past, its only purpose was to transmit information vital to the survival of the species. Some people still think that's the only thing it should be used for, but most folks today use it mostly for fun."

It is rare for Judi to send me this sort of email, a forwarded, generally circulating email; this may in fact be the first time. Given the timing, I'd like to take it as Judi's response to my telling her I needed an ending to my paper.

While Judi probably sent me this message "mostly for fun," I'd like to take the equation of email and the penis way too seriously, to treat it as a theoretical contribution to the topic of feminism and rhetoric. I'd like us to read its rhetoric seriously. By its rhetoric I mean everything from its dissemination, to its tone, to the odd fact that it is a list not of ten but of eleven reasons why email is like a penis. (Eleven seems to me a very odd number, one that screams "one too many," one that's asking for the reader to lop one off.)

As reason # 6 tells us, email today is more likely to be used for dissemination than insemination. Whatever my fantasies of a private relation, one of the things that characterizes email is the ease with which writing can be put into wide and speedy circulation. The "ending" Judi sent us, this example of a widely circulating message, can remind us that an econstructed sisterhood is one inevitably disseminated beyond my fantasies of a cozy closed circuit.

This multiply forwarded email recalls another important sense of "sisterhood," one that picks up, forwards, and transforms the feminist rhetoric. "Sisterhood" was always meant to be a broad relation, one that was not private, restricted to either our natural or even our chosen sisters, an open rather than a closed community. Sending me this message, just in time to get it included in this paper, Judi makes me see our relation as part of a larger econstructed circuit.

The message is quasi-feminist in tone. Its playful, critical relation to the penis suggests a female perspective, not just female but with a critical distance on phallocentrism ("Those who have it think that those who don't are somehow inferior"). The message could be taken as an assertive, playful feminist statement bonding a circuit of women.

But the message is also ironic. While the content is distant from and critical of an investment in email, the fact that it is itself an email message means that writer and reader bond in a contradictory relation. This combination of ironic distance notwithstanding continuing investment may well be the rhetoric of women bonding over and through our ambivalent relation to men.

Although Judi did not author this email she sent me, although she literally did not add anything to the message, there nonetheless is something of hers to read there—not in the message itself but in the address. The "To:" line of the heading contains three e-addresses: at the same time Judi forwarded this message to me she also sent it to two other women, her best friend, and her exhusband's girlfriend, who happens also to be named Jane (Judi sometimes refers to her as "the other Jane"). Judi has developed quite a nice relationship to that Jane, a relationship that in fact developed and largely exists on email. Judi's ex-husband is troubled by this bond.

I am of course Judi's literal sister; best girlfriends are often figured as "sisters"; but what sort of sister is "the other Jane"? To answer that question, I turn to an esteemed feminist theorist. Gayatri Spivak once told me that women who have slept with the same man are called cocksisters. Now I have to confess that I don't know where Gayatri got the term nor what all it is meant to imply. But with a message telling me that email is like a penis, I am prompted to speculate that there may well be a connection between what I'm here calling econstructed sisterhood and what Spivak calls cocksisters.

Judi's relation to the other Jane is literally "econstructed": they got close by writing email. Judi has, it turns out, econstructed two relations, one with me and one with this other Jane. These two econstructed sisterhoods have something in common beyond the coincidence of name: both relations involve women connecting across rivalry. Judi and me, literal sisters, negotiate sibling rivalry; Judi and the other Jane bond across sexual rivalry.

Back in the days of cozy "sisterhood," "sisters" (who later became cultural feminists and lesbian separatists) were valued not only because we were alike but also and importantly because we were different from men, a difference implicating technology and the phallus. The phallus, technology, theory, and rhetoric were all male, and the fantasy of sisterhood was a fantasy of unmediated connection. "Econstructed sisterhood" demands a way of thinking about women bonding beyond the cultural feminist fantasy of women's antiphallic, natural sameness.

I said earlier that I thought what we needed in feminism was not so much an ethics of difference between women but a rhetoric. At the end of this paper, I'm still at the beginning of that question. In view of that as yet unimaginable rhetoric, I've posted the example of my email correspondence with my sister. And in lieu of a conclusion I've brought the message my sister forwarded last Monday as a theorization of email and gender.

While it may be only coincidental that Judi and the other Jane have an econstructed relation, Judi's meta-email suggests a stronger, more theoretical connection. The complicated tone of ironic distance despite real attachment for both penis and email in that message bonds its circuit of readers in an econstructed sisterhood that may also be an instance of a rhetorical bond I am amused to call cocksisterhood.

■　■　■

Thus ends the paper proper. After I presented it at the English Institute, about a dozen people said they wanted me to write and tell them what happened in Minnesota the next week. Here's what happened:

Reading the paper with my sister and mother in the audience was really scary. I delivered the entire paper without once looking in their direction. I was afraid that if I looked at them I would not be able to continue reading; I was more afraid of what I would see on their faces. While I generally deliver papers slowly, wanting the audience to catch every word I have written, I read this paper hyper-slowly: I was stalling. I took a sip of water between each paragraph because I was afraid to go on.

The audience was stunningly quiet. Someone who was there later told me that she thought the audience was afraid of what I might say, what might happen. It was as if the audience saw me at the precipice and held its breath, expecting me to jump.

It was in fact an event; it felt live. In the paper I had written of a tightrope walk without a net, and that was how I felt—as if at any moment I could plunge. The risk did not seem academic.

So, you may be wondering, how did they take it? What did they think? ("They," of course, are Judi and Mom.)

Judi loved it. I felt my gift to her was a great success. She seemed expansive and looked radiant afterward. She asked me for a copy of the paper, told me she liked it even better upon reading it, circulated copies to friends, including Shawna and the other Jane. (She forwarded to me the email Shawna wrote her after reading the paper; so I know that while a bit put off by the academic vocabulary, Shawna thinks Judi fortunate to have a sister like me.) Judi also confirmed that she did indeed forward me the "email is like a penis" list because she hoped it might help me write the conclusion.

Mom, on the other hand, seemed tense after the paper. We embraced awkwardly when I returned to my seat, and she left shortly thereafter. I spent the next day at her house, and it was as if nothing had happened, which was both a relief and demoralizing.

The next Saturday, during our first phone call since the talk, Mom and I had a fight, the worst fight in years. Having taken the risk of complaining publicly about her phone calls, I could not bear finding myself in a call where nothing seemed to have changed; so I criticized her directly. Whereas in writing the talk I had carefully composed my criticism of her, editing out as much of my angry excesses as I could, in the call I said everything I had edited out of the talk, and more. We found ourselves in an increasingly bitter exchange of reciprocal accusations. The call ended with us both still in full anger. Mom said that she was hanging up and that I had better call next week.

The following Saturday Mom was exemplary in her attentiveness, asking me questions about my life, questions she seemed to have jotted down upon reading my latest email to Judi. As I write this afterword, that is my most recent contact with Mom.

If this seems too cozy an ending, it probably means I am once again closing the circuits of sisterhood. So let me end by speaking of another member of my family who was present at that event, someone I have not yet mentioned in this paper.

While I told you Mom was sitting next to Judi, I didn't tell you that on the other side of Judi sat Stacy, my brother's wife. In retrospect it seems remarkable that in a discussion of various forms of sisterhood, of mediated, and tense, and rivalrous sisterhoods, of women bonding across their relations to men, I neglected to mention my sister-in-law.

Whereas Judi and I now have different family names (she has kept her ex-husband's name), Stacy has become a Gallop. When I said Judi was "my only sister," was I intentionally excluding Stacy? Am I trying to reduce my family to a cozy, childhood version of it, only counting the "blood relatives"? Am I rejecting the constructed sister-in-law for the natural sister, by only counting the latter?

It is not, believe me, because I don't like Stacy. I like Stacy enormously, think she's wonderful, appreciate her sensitivity and wisdom. I often say that Stacy is my favorite person in my family, feeling this a rather clever if pointed joke. Right now I'm realizing that I don't really understand the joke.

I am realizing that I have some resistance to counting her as a "sister." I suspect that over the nearly twenty years she's been part of my family I have often slighted Stacy in just this way. And as I close this paper, I'd like to begin thinking about what *that* means.

Afterwords

■ ■ ■

The Chance for Something to Happen

Most of the chapters of this book were, at least originally, occasional. I have never really understood why occasional writing is held to be a deconsidered genre. . . . (Actually, I do understand, but I don't share the prejudice. I prefer the gossipy grain of situated writing to the academic sublime.)

These words could have been written about *this* book. They were, however, written about a book published a decade ago, a bit before the earliest pieces in *Anecdotal Theory*. I found them in Nancy K. Miller's preface to her 1991 volume of essays, *Getting Personal*.[1] I share Miller's textual preference for situated grain over abstract sublime.

The last essay of the present book led me to express and defend my preference for occasional writing: "I stress the 'occasional' nature of my talk . . . because I believe in the fertility of the specific as the site of productive thinking. . . . occasional pieces are . . . rhetorical sites where discourse is knotted to the extradiscursive, to the here and now, to real life." While "Econstructing Sisterhood" is the most blatantly occasional (written for my sister's birthday), all the essays in this volume could be considered occasional pieces; all were written for particular academic events. Like *Getting Personal, Anecdotal Theory* is a collection of occasional theory.

Explaining what she values in the occasional, Miller uses language similar to what this book uses to value the anecdotal: "In the notion of the occasional I have . . . wanted to seize the fallout of event: the chance for something to happen in the wedge of unpredictability not yet foreclosed by my own (rhetorically predictable) . . . discourse" (Miller, xi–xii). Both the anecdotal and the occasional are places where discourse responds to event. Like Fineman's anecdotal, Miller's occasional involves a dynamic of opening (the wedge) and closure (foreclosed). Although closure seems inevitable (not *yet* foreclosed), Miller seeks opening; her particular word for such opening is "unpredictability." Miller's predictable discourse is like Fineman's teleological narration ("a story whose conclusion is already written"). The occasional opens predictable discourse to the unpredictability of event.

Like Miller, I have wanted to seize the fallout of event; that is the point of anecdotal theory. I hope the anecdotal can wedge open my own theoretically predictable discourse. Above all, through the anecdotal, I want to leave open the chance for something to happen.

The occasional and the anecdotal are not, to be sure, identical. Anecdotes recount incidents: in them discourse *follows* event, tries to capture the event in language. Occasional writing, on the other hand, *precedes* event: discourse tries to prepare for, to suit itself in advance to, an event. Whereas occasional writing is always, in a way, prefatory, the anecdotal is always a sort of "afterword" (language that comes after).

Knotted as they are to event, both the anecdotal and the occasional moor discourse to history. Yet their differing temporal relations to the event give them different relations to history. While anecdotes may be the basic unit of historiography, occasional writing (participant in the event) is itself historic.

At the beginning of "The Stories," I mentioned that as the present volume moves toward "Econstructing Sisterhood" it marks time more precisely, as if trying to get ever closer to the moment. One might say that the volume moves from anecdotal to occasional theory. Beyond theory which responds to event, I would like to move toward theory which takes its place in history, in the unpredictability of event. Occasional theory offers the chance for something to happen . . . for something to happen *to theory*.

Yet in a book like this, the occasional necessarily becomes anecdotal again. Once published, occasional writing is after the event, part of the account of the event. In order to make a book of occasional writing, the occasion must be recounted.

In an afterword to one of the essays in *Getting Personal,* Miller theorizes about recounting such occasions: "The narrative of these occasions is necessarily locational: it is what happens to theory in the flesh of practice, in the social spaces of institutional life" (97). In the narrative of these occasions, the occasion becomes anecdote. And in the "after-words" that are our books of occasional theory, something "happens to theory"; theory is anecdotalized.

Anecdotalized theory is, as Miller suggests, not the "academic sublime," but theory situated. "In the social spaces of institutional life" (where things happen to theory). Or as she so evocatively puts it: "theory in the flesh of practice."

The Anecdotal Feminist

In the notion of the occasional I have also wanted to seize the fallout of event: the chance for something to happen in the wedge of unpredictability not yet foreclosed by my own (rhetorically predictable) feminist discourse.

When I quoted this passage a page or so ago, I left out the word "feminist." I wanted to focus on Miller's theorization of the occasional, and it seemed to make the exposition clearer to leave feminism out. In my quest for theoretical clarity, I performed an abstraction, simplifying what is tangled together in Miller's practice of theory. In *Getting Personal,* the occasional is consistently connected to feminism, but it is not clear exactly what the connection is.

The preface tells us Miller originally called the volume "The Occasional Feminist." This suggests not only that the occasional was central to her project but that the occasional was centrally connected to feminism. The book's current subtitle uses the phrase "Feminist Occasions." Although this phrase resembles the old title, noun and adjective positions are reversed. Whereas earlier "feminist" was a noun qualified by "occasional," now the "occasions" seem primary, modified by a secondary feminism. While the subtitle puts "feminist" on the side of the events, the sentence from the preface puts "feminist" on the side of the discourse which events give us a chance to open up. In *Getting Personal,* both the occasional and the discourse it opens up can be feminist. If I am here interrogating Miller's text on the relation between feminism and the occasional, it is because I feel I ought, before finishing *this* book, to pin down the relation between feminism and anecdotal theory.

Does Miller consider her preference for the occasional to be feminist? Although she doesn't say, one certainly could mount an argument for that position—feminists (or is it women?) prefer the situated to the abstract. But as I imagine the argument, I hear Miller's phrase "my own (rhetorically predictable) feminist discourse." Reminded that Miller locates the occasional as what disrupts the predictability of feminist argument, I realize that the argument I am generating is too automatic, too predictable (written, as Miller says elsewhere, by "a feminist computer" [122]).

The temptation to identify Miller's textual preference as feminist recalls the urge to identify a feminist sexual preference. That tendency was all the rage in the seventies feminism that was formative for Miller and me. Many feminists (both lesbian and heterosexual) now feel that it was a mistake to attempt to label as feminist what anyone did "in the flesh of practice."

So-called feminist sexuality turned out to bear all too much of a resemblance to traditional feminine behavior. When we label a style of practice (sexual or otherwise) feminist, we may well be returning to the most predictable sort of gendering. Such gendering is the subject of the first essay in the present volume. "The Teacher's Breasts" examines how the effort to identify a feminist style of teaching results in the prescription of appropriately gendered *feminine* behavior. In that essay, what the feminist teacher calls an "incident" wedges open the predictably gendered theory of feminist pedagogy—precisely the effect on feminist discourse that Miller would want from event.

Getting Personal never genders the practice of occasional writing. At one point in the book, Miller does, however, undergo what she calls the "temptation" to gender a writing practice. This temptation is both fleeting and marginal (it occurs in a footnote). And, to be sure, Miller resolves to resist such temptation. I nevertheless mention it here because the writing practice she would gender turns out to be the anecdote: "In a first rough cut, it does seem, however, that . . . the anecdote . . . has been a way for some men to experiment with self-representation while writing critical theory. But the use of anecdote also characterizes the essays of black women writers like Alice Walker and June Jordan, so one will have to resist the temptation to gender the anecdote—including, of course, my own" (Miller, 27). Miller can't quite suppress her urge to "gender the anecdote" as male, yet in the very next sentence she corrects herself by naming women writers who use anecdote.[2]

The dramatic tensions in this note make for quite interesting reading, and a lot could be said about it. But the note lays particular claim to my interest here because what Miller is talking about is not simply the anecdote but is actually anecdotal theory ("the anecdote has been a way to experiment while writing theory"). Whereas Miller genders anecdotal theory male, I would want to go the other way, making it a womanly alternative to phallic theory. The contradiction between Miller's gendering of it and my own dissuades me from any attempt to gender the anecdote. Instead, it seems like it might be more productive to anecdotalize gender.

Consider, for example, gender in "The Teacher's Breasts": "student lines up with male, teacher with female. This is not the order of theoretical models . . . but rather comes from the actual relations at play." Coming "from the actual relations at play," gender in this essay is occasional and wedges open the more predictable gendering of feminist theoretical models. The very same anecdotal gendering (male student, female teacher) appears in "Knot a Love Story," where it has a similar effect of destabilizing positions ("I felt like I had switched genders"). As it appears in these two essays from 1992, such anecdotal gendering is situational and performative.[3]

A month or so ago, as I faced writing this closing piece for *Anecdotal Theory,* I fantasized concluding the book with something called "An Anecdotal Theory of Gender." I would use the anecdotal considerations of gender in the book to counter a too predictable, too fixed, too essentialist theory of gender. But as I imagined writing what would be an impressive theoretical conclusion, something in me resisted moving from anecdote to theory, fixing the anecdotal in a final, abstract, generalizable form. Despite my resistance, I nonetheless longed for such an ending, a grand theoretical finale.

Concluding the book with a theory of gender would make *Anecdotal Theory* definitively, monumentally feminist. And I can find myself wishing for that because I worry that anecdotal theory is not recognizably feminist.

Most of the chapters of this book were, at least originally, feminist. The essays intervene in feminist debates, using the anecdotal to wedge open a too predictable feminist theory. The first essay engages with feminist discourse on pedagogy; the last contributes to an ongoing discussion in feminist theory about differences between women. Along the way I tangle both incidentally and theoretically with the feminist theorization of sexual harassment.

Bringing the essays together as a book, I have wanted to emphasize not the specific topics and questions (pedagogy, sexuality, differences between women) but the method of theorizing, the practice I'm calling anecdotal theory. I'm not sure that the style of theory I prefer is particularly feminist. And as I write this final piece about the book as a whole, I can feel defensive that the book is only anecdotally feminist.

Theory in the Flesh of Practice

> The narrative of these occasions is . . . what happens to theory in the flesh of practice, in the social spaces of institutional life.

I want to talk for a moment about "the social spaces of institutional life." A good example of such a space is the yearly Modern Language Association convention. Three of the essays collected in *Getting Personal* are MLA talks, as are two of the essays collected here. The MLA is a place for occasional theory, a place where people present theoretical work, but also a social space, a place where people socialize with colleagues.

I gave my first MLA talk in 1975, on a panel chaired by Nancy Miller. She put out a call for papers; I submitted an abstract; that was where I first met Nancy. We've been friends for a long time now, and when we are both at MLA, we get together and talk, usually over food.

In one of the MLA talks I've included here ("Castration Anxiety and the Unemployed Ph.D."), I say I'd like to "cross the discursive line between the two MLAS." While in that paper "the two MLAS" refers to panels where we do theory and panels where we discuss the fate of the profession, I would like now to take crossing the line between the two MLAS as a general image for the project of anecdotal theory. I'd like to cross the discursive line between the intellectual work we present in our panels and the talk we do in the bars, restaurants, and lobbies of the MLA.

As an emblem of that crossing, I've chosen to end this book by putting my writing in conversation with Nancy Miller. I would like *Anecdotal Theory* to have the range of my conversations with Nancy, to move from anecdote to theory and back again with the ease and benefit of those conversations. I put *Anecdotal Theory* in dialogue with Miller's *Getting Personal* here because what I mean by "my conversations with Nancy" is not just our breakfasts at MLA or our phone calls but our books and essays.

I take my conversation with Nancy as an emblem not because it is unique but because it is representative. There are other people I meet with regularly at MLA or in other social spaces of institutional life, intellectual colleagues who are also friends. And I am hardly the only one who has such relations; they are in fact legion. You can glimpse them all around you in the bars of MLA hotels or in the acknowledgments and footnotes of scholarly writing.

You can also glimpse them here and there in this book. Take, for example, "The Personal and the Professional," an essay which argues in fact for crossing a line (or "walking the line") very much like the line between "the two MLAs." Here is part of that essay's explanation of what moved me to write it: "I began talking to my friends around the country, feminist academics of my generation, and discovered that a large number of us had had sexual relations with teachers either as undergraduates or as graduate students. . . . I was . . . concerned that an entire stretch of experience was being denied, consigned to silence." "Consigned to silence" here does not in fact mean no one is talking about it. Rather it refers to a discursive line: things discussed informally that do not pass into formal discourse. Referring to personal conversations with "my friends around the country, academics," the essay crosses that discursive line in order to bring into theoretical discourse what is whispered in the social spaces of institutional life.

The same sort of socializing is also behind the essay "Resisting Reasonableness." That essay bases its theory in a story told to me over coffee. The woman told me her story in response to reading *Feminist Accused of Sexual Harassment.* Anecdotal theory here is a circuit which passes from anecdote to theory to anecdote to theory in a spiral of knowledge and talk. Anecdotal theory here is also a circuit that passes through different individuals, exchanging anecdotes and theory, in writing but also in the flesh.

We might take my last essay in this book, "Econstructing Sisterhood," as an exploration of this transindividual circuit of theory. Or we might take the first essay in *Getting Personal,* the title essay of the collection. "Getting Personal" reads and responds to other critics' personal writing, setting them in dialogue with each other, a dialogue which passes seamlessly between anecdote and theorizing. As if Nancy had hosted a get-together of intellectual colleagues, the effect is to create in writing something like a social space.

One of the invitees is Eve Sedgwick, present in the guise of her 1987 essay "A Poem Is Being Written." Miller quotes from Sedgwick: "Part of the motivation behind my work has been a fantasy that readers or hearers would be variously . . . stimulated to write accounts 'like' this one of their own, and share those." Miller then comments: "What Sedgwick records here . . . is the desire for a response. . . . This might take the form, for instance, of more personal criticism . . . but also of gestures, not predetermined, that would bring out other voices from their own shadows."[4]

Sedgwick's "fantasy" is of an exchange, creating the possibility of a circuit. As other voices come out from the shadows, more and more writing would cross the line between the personal and the professional. These "not predetermined" gestures are precisely not predictable. What Miller and Sedgwick here imagine is something in writing that would be like an occasion.

Sharing anecdotes is a familiar mode of social interaction, one that typically takes place in person. At the beginning of "The Stories," I noted that my essays tended to use the gambits of oral storytelling. The essays like to conjure up a here and now where storyteller and hearer are together in the flesh. Occasional theory is about trying to bring the unpredictability and responsiveness of the flesh into writing. Abstract, disembodied theory, theory in no place or time, dreams of being the last word. Occasional, anecdotal theory, theory in the flesh of practice, speaks with the desire for a response.

Anecdotal Theory

1 Barbara Christian, "The Race for Theory," in Linda Kauffman, ed., *Gender and Theory: Dialogues on Feminist Criticism* (New York: Basil Blackwell, 1989), p. 226.

2 Joel Fineman, "The History of the Anecdote: Fiction and Friction," in *The Subjectivity Effect in Western Literary Tradition: Essays Toward the Release of Shakespeare's Will* (Cambridge, Mass: MIT Press, 1991), p. 67. I am grateful to Nancy K. Miller for directing my attention to Fineman's essay.

3 Christian's "The Race for Theory" was originally written for a conference at the University of California, Berkeley entitled "Minority Discourse" and held on May 29–31, 1986. Fineman's "The History of the Anecdote: Fiction and Friction" was originally delivered at a conference on "The New Historicism: The Boundaries of Social History," Stanford University, October 9, 1987. As for their collegiality, it must be said that while both taught at Berkeley, Fineman was in the English Department whereas Christian was in Afro-American Studies.

4 My sense of the moment, my imagining of Fineman on a Berkeley path in the eighties, is made poignant by the knowledge that Joel Fineman died an untimely death in 1989.

5 Ellen is the actual name of a student who, I am happy to report, has already fulfilled the promise of brilliance that so inspired me back in that 1992

classroom. Already an accomplished theoretical writer and academic, she published her first book with a university press a few years ago (E. L. McCallum, *Object Lessons: How to Do Things with Fetishism* [Albany, N.Y.: SUNY Press, 1999]).

6   Jacques Derrida, *De la grammatologie* (Paris: Minuit, 1967), p. 231, translation mine.

7   "We would like to reach the point of a certain exteriority.... To exceed the metaphysical orb is an attempt to get out of the rut (*orbita*)" (pp. 231–32, translation mine). Derrida uses the word "ornière," which means "rut" and places the Latin "orbita" in parenthesis after it ("ornière" derives, if a bit illegitimately, from "orbita"). The published English translation renders "ornière" as "orbit" and loses the sense of getting out of a rut. See Jacques Derrida, *Of Grammatology*, trans. Gayatri Chakravorty Spivak (Baltimore: Johns Hopkins University Press, 1976), pp. 161–62.

8   Fineman, p. 78, n. 24. It is noteworthy that this suggestion of the anecdote's erotic nature appears in Fineman's endnotes. In fact, while there is a good bit of sex in Fineman's "History," it's pretty much all relegated to the notes. (Fineman's notes are in themselves remarkable by being as long as his text, if not longer. We would in fact have to call his notes "exorbitant.") By consigning the erotics of the anecdote to the endnotes, Fineman is not so much repressing it as enacting its particular seduction. Although the anecdotes behind theory are most often not published at all, when they are they tend to be found in the margins of the text—prefaces and footnotes, the more personal, less public zones.

9   Catharine A. MacKinnon, *Sexual Harassment of Working Women: A Case of Sex Discrimination* (New Haven: Yale University Press, 1979), p. xii.

1. The Teacher's Breasts

1   Margo Culley and Catherine Portuges, "Introduction," in *Gendered Subjects: The Dynamics of Feminist Teaching* (Boston: Routledge and Kegan Paul, 1985), p. 5.

2   Margo Culley, Arlyn Diamond, Lee Edwards, Sara Lennox, Catherine Portuges, "The Politics of Nurturance," pp. 11–20.

3   Robert J. Bezucha, "Feminist Pedagogy as a Subversive Activity," pp. 81–95; Diedrick Snoek, "A Male Feminist in a Women's College Classroom," pp. 136–43; John Schilb, "Pedagogy of the Oppressors?" pp. 253–64.

4   Or add "and men" in parenthesis, a gesture which suggests an inclusion that would change nothing.

5   For example, see Culley, "Anger and Authority in the Introductory Wom-

en's Studies Classroom," pp. 213–14, and Bezucha, "Feminist Pedagogy as a Subversive Activity," pp. 88–89.

6   See, for example, "The Politics of Nurturance," pp. 17–19. For a similar celebration of the erotics of feminist pedagogy, see Madeleine Grumet, *Bitter Milk: Women and Teaching* (Amherst: University of Massachusetts Press, 1988).

7   Judith McDaniel, "Is There Room for Me in the Closet? Or, My Life as the Only Lesbian Professor," pp. 130–35.

8   Rich, "Taking Women Students Seriously," in *Gendered Subjects*, p. 26.

9   Susan Miller, "Cross Country," *West Coast Plays* 1 (Fall 1977): 56–57; recounted in Keyssar, p. 118.

10 This last word is meant to resonate with the title of Keyssar's course: Feminist Theater Ensemble.

11 I am indebted to Fran Bartkowski for this association, which she offered me in August 1992.

2. *The Lecherous Professor*

1   For a highly readable and generally accurate account of those details, I refer you to Margaret Talbot, "A Most Dangerous Method," *Lingua Franca* 4.2 (Jan./Feb. 1994): 1, 24–40.

2   Ellen Bravo, English Department Sexual Harassment Workshop, University of Wisconsin, Milwaukee, January 28, 1993.

3   This sentence is worded ("manifest/latent") to make this piece of theorizing about ideology and writing an addendum to and elaboration of Freudian interpretation. I'm suggesting that the conscious goal of stylistic ease can serve as a means by which pieces of ideology that would be consciously rejected by the author can pass into discourse. The repressed here is not sex but sexual prejudice (assuming we could distinguish those two). This notion of the correlation between stylistic grace and retrograde ideology also recalls a formulation by Joanna Russ: "Something that has been worked on by others in the same culture . . . provides a writer with material that has been distilled . . . and . . . clarified. . . . what [the writer] does will be neither tentative nor crude . . . it can simply be done well." "What Can a Heroine Do? Or Why Women Can't Write," in Susan Koppelman Cornillon, ed., *Images of Women in Fiction: Feminist Perspectives* (Bowling Green, Ohio: Bowling Green University Popular Press, 1973), p. 11. Russ suggests that those who reproduce dominant ideology will write more smoothly; I am going on to suggest that those who attempt to write smoothly may find themselves unwittingly reproducing dominant ideology.

4 "Collegian" also suggests the victim's youth.

5 Barry M. Dank, letter to the author, April 22, 1994.

6 Correlatively the first chapter—which bears the book's subtitle as its title, "Sexual Harassment on Campus"—is subtitled "The State of the Art."

7 I am grateful to attorney Walter F. Kelly for pointing this out to me. He is, of course, in no way responsible for my interpretations.

8 Antonio J. Califa, Memorandum to Regional Civil Rights Directors, Regions I–X, Office for Civil Rights, United States Department of Education (Washington, D.C., August 31, 1981), quoted in *The Lecherous Professor,* p. 19.

9 Guidelines included as an appendix to *The Lecherous Professor,* pp. 189–91.

10 Billie Wright Dziech, "The Bedeviling Issue of Sexual Harassment," *Chronicle of Higher Education,* December 8, 1993, p. A48. I am grateful to Dick Blau for bringing this article to my attention.

3. The Personal and the Professional: Walking the Line

1 Margo Culley and Catherine Portuges, "Introduction," in *Gendered Subjects: The Dynamics of Feminist Teaching* (Boston: Routledge and Kegan Paul, 1985), p. 5.

2 Catharine A. MacKinnon, *Sexual Harassment of Working Women: A Case of Sex Discrimination* (New Haven: Yale University Press, 1979), p. xii, emphasis added.

3 Adrienne Rich, "Taking Women Students Seriously," in *On Lies, Secrets, and Silence: Selected Prose 1966-1978* (New York: Norton, 1979), pp. 237–45.

4 Adrienne Rich, "Compulsory Heterosexuality and Lesbian Existence," in Ann Snitow, Christine Stansell, and Sharon Thompson, eds., *Powers of Desire: The Politics of Sexuality* (New York: Monthly Review Press, 1983), pp. 177–205.

4. Resisting Reasonableness

1 This paper was originally written for a February 1998 symposium at the Center for Lesbian and Gay Studies at CUNY Graduate Center. I want to thank Jill Dolan and Nancy Miller for that invitation. I'd also like to thank my dissertators Astrid Henry and Gary Weissman for their critical readings of this essay.

The Stories

1 Hegel provides the great example of a history where everything is determined by the logical progress of an idea. Hegel is Fineman's example in the

passage quoted here, but the tendency he typifies is not aberrant but inherent in historiography.

2 In this discussion of historicism and what I will here call an "other historicism," it is worth noting that Fineman's "History of the Anecdote" is in fact meant also to be a discussion of the mid-eighties literary critical school called New Historicism. The present consideration of historicism has numerous points of intersection with Fineman's attempt to historicize the New Historicism.

5. A Tale of Two Jacques

1 For a dozen years I have clearly remembered reading this, in the fall of 1979, in the anthology *Female Sexuality: New Psychoanalytic Views,* edited by Janine Chasseguet-Smirgel (Ann Arbor: University of Michigan Press, 1970), although I did not remember which essay it was in. I remember that this passage brought a shock of recognition. However, going back now over and over through the book, I cannot find the passage. The closest thing I can find is Joyce McDougall's discussion of "The Masculine Woman" in "Homosexuality in Women," pp. 178–82, which seems familiar but not exactly right. Perhaps the clear memory is a screen memory or the panicked inability to find it is symptomatic, or both. In any case, I give up.

2 Jane Gallop, "The Ladies' Man," *Diacritics* 6.4 (1976): 30.

3 I thought this session was called "Lacan *and* Derrida Revisited." Reading the program I saw that, where I expected an "and," there is a slash.

4 Barbara Johnson, "The Frame of Reference: Poe, Lacan, Derrida," *Yale French Studies* 55–56 (1977): 459.

5 Jacques Derrida, *La Carte postale: de Socrate à Freud et au delà* (Paris: Flammarion, 1980), p. 488, all translations mine.

6 Johnson, "The Frame of Reference," p. 472.

7 Jane Gallop, *Reading Lacan* (Ithaca: Cornell University Press, 1985), pp. 64, 65, 73.

8 Here I think of the film *Dead Ringers,* which seems to have something to say about this relation.

7. Dating Derrida in the Nineties

1 Originally entitled "La Question du style," the paper was first published in the proceedings of that colloquium, *Nietzsche Aujourd'hui?, V. 1 Intensités* (Paris: Union Generale d'Editions [Collection 10/18], 1973), pp. 235–87. In 1976, retitled *Éperons: Les styles de Nietzsche,* the paper was republished as a book in four languages—the original French alongside translations into

Italian, English, and German (Venice: Corbo e Fiore Editori). The French version alone was published as a book in 1978 by Flammarion. The French and English versions from the 1976 four-language edition were published in 1979 by the University of Chicago Press as *Spurs: Nietzsche's Styles / Éperons: Les Styles de Nietzsche*. The English translation by Barbara Harlow for the 1976 four-language edition reappears in the 1979 American bilingual edition. All references, unless otherwise noted, will be to the 1979 bilingual edition.

2 *The Gay Science*, 363, quoted in *Spurs*, pp.154–55, n. 9/14.

3 p. 96. The numbering of the paragraphs is in the French text as well as the Italian and German translations; it is oddly omitted from the English translation (see 1976, 76–77).

4 Alexander Argyros, "Daughters of the Desert," *Diacritics* 10.3 (September 1980): 33.

5 Alice Jardine, *Gynesis: Configurations of Woman and Modernity* (Ithaca: Cornell University Press, 1985), p. 193, n. 64.

6 I saw a movie poster with the line: "In 1866 a woman had two choices . . . she could be a wife or she could be a whore." Advertisement for *The Ballad of Little Jo*, by Maggie Greenwald, 1993.

7 pp. 84–85. Italicization and brackets, Derrida's. Harlow adds quotation marks to her translation of the italicization. The word "époque" appearing twice in this passage is the same found in the earlier "La 'femme'—le mot fait époque."

8 I am grateful for discussion with Marcus Bullock, of the UWM German department, about Nietzsche's various words for "women." Marcus is not responsible for my inevitable misuses of the observations on these words he so generously shared with me.

9 The 1979 French/English edition of *Spurs* is divided into thirteen sections, each headed by a title. The title of the section which ends with "Frauenzimmer" is "Veils/Sails"; the next section is called "Truths." In the 1978 French edition, each section begins on a new page and the section titles appear in the running heads. Here in the monolingual edition the sections are chapters, perhaps in order to make the paper into a "book." The sections are in neither the 1976 four-language edition nor the original 1973 publication of "La Question du style."

10 The English translation makes it hard to follow Derrida's emphasis on the verb "prendre." This verb appears for the German "einnehmen" in the quoted French translation of Nietzsche. The quoted English translation of Nietzsche renders "einnehmen" with "win," but the English translation of Derrida uses "pin down" (and a bit later, "capture") for "prendre," making

it difficult to catch Derrida's repetition of Nietzsche's verb. The simplest English equivalent of "prendre" would be "take."

11 Cf. Alice Walker, *In Search of Our Mothers' Gardens* (New York: Harcourt Brace, 1983), p. 376: "Racism decrees that if *they* are now women (years ago they were ladies, but fashions change) then black women must, perforce, be something else. (While they were 'ladies,' black women could be 'women,' and so on.)"

Afterwords

1 Nancy K. Miller, *Getting Personal: Feminist Occasions and Other Auto-biographical Acts* (New York: Routledge, 1991), pp. xi.

2 The particular combination in this note of black women writers and new historicist men returns me to my opening juxtaposition of Barbara Christian and Joel Fineman. The latter in fact appears in a part of this passage that I elided: "the anecdote revived and reauthorized most recently by the new historicism, but long a rhetorical staple of a whole range of discursive practices (brilliantly analyzed by Joel Fineman in his 'History of the Anecdote'), has been a way for some men to experiment" (27).

3 This occasional or anecdotalized gender has, I realize, a lot in common with Judith Butler's notion of performative gender (*Gender Trouble* [New York: Routledge, 1990]). In "Knot a Love Story," the anecdotal gender occasions language such as "play-acting" and "drag performance."

4 *Getting Personal*, p. 24. Miller quotes from Eve Kosofsky Sedgwick, "A Poem Is Being Written," *Representations* 17 (Winter 1987): 137.

Castration (*cont.*)
the symbolic order, 132. *See also*
Anxiety

Chodorow, Nancy J., 24, 34

Christian, Barbara, 1–3, 7, 9–10, 165
n.3, 171 n.2

Class, 49, 59, 116, 119–20, 125

Closet, metaphor of, 39–41, 69. *See
also* Homophobia

Deconstruction, 1, 3, 7–9, 37, 106, 113,
138, 145; and feminism, 4–5, 9–10;
and psychoanalysis, 10–11; and sexual harassment policy, 38–39. *See
also* Derrida, Jacques

Derrida, Jacques: *Le facteur de la ver-
ite*, 11, 93–99; and feminism, 87, 89,
112–14, 119, 123–26; on Friedrich
Nietzsche, 3, 112–26, 170 n.10; *Of
Grammatology*, 7–9, 166 n.7; on
Jacques Lacan, 10–11, 83–84, 93–99;
Spurs, 3–4, 87–90, 112–26, 169 n.1,
170 n.10. *See also* Deconstruction;
Dissemination

Desire: feminism and, 114, 146; and
power, 63, 129; and respect, 65; for a
response, 164. *See also* Anecdote(s):
and desire; Pedagogy: and desire

Discrimination. *see* Sexual harassment: as discrimination

Dissemination, 145, 149. *See also* Derrida, Jacques

Domesticity, 99, 139, 142. *See also*
Family

Dziech, Billie Wright, 36–50

Education. *See* Feminist pedagogy;
Pedagogy; Sexual harassment:
and education; Women: and
education

Email, 91–92; and feminism, 141–54;
and gender, 151

Empiricism, 8, 134

Eroticism: and power struggle, 94,
107; and "theory," 11. *See also* Anec-
dote(s): as erotic; Pedagogy: eroticism of

Essentialism, 90, 122–26, 161

Ethics: in feminism, 143, 151; in teaching, 73, 104. *See also* Morality

Ethnocentrism, 139

Experience: of the academic jobseeker, 128–29; as basis for theory,
2, 14–18, 20, 22, 163; and feminist
epistemology, 18–19, 52, 56; men's,
32; and pedagogy, 24, 32, 71–72, 75,
104–6, 110; and psychoanalysis, 130;
women's, 9, 56. *See also* Sexual
harassment: and experience

Family: extended, 153–54; and feminism, 142; and generational relations, 4; oedipal structure of, 96–
97; of origin, 142, 145, 147. *See also*
Domesticity; Sisterhood

Feminism: and abstraction, 159; and
anger, 146–47; antisex vs. pro-sex,
60–66; bad-girl vs. good-girl, 28–
29, 35; and castration, 132–33; cultural, 151; as ethnocentric, 139; and
men, 24, 27–35, 57, 60; in the 1970s,
3–5, 27, 45, 94, 113–14, 123–26, 139;
in the 1980s, 3, 6, 24, 33, 40, 60, 114,
139; in the 1990s, 4, 49, 63, 113–114,
119, 124–26; and non-feminist
women, 138, 139, 141, 143; and pornography, 60–61; and sibling rivalry, 139–41. *See also* Anecdote(s):
and feminism; Deconstruction:
and feminism; Ethics: in feminism;

Feminist pedagogy; History: and feminism; Method: feminist; Psychoanalysis: and feminism; Rhetoric: and feminism; Sexual harassment: and feminism; Sisterhood; Women's Studies

Feminist pedagogy, 6, 18–19, 21, 23–35, 54–56, 62–65; and femininity 25, 29, 33–35, 159–60; and men, 23–35; and mother-daughter relations, 24, 35; and the personal, 5–6, 18–19, 23–24, 54–57, 64. *See also* Breast(s); Chodorow, Nancy J.; Experience: and pedagogy; Knowledge: women's; Lesbians: and teaching; Pedagogy; Women: and education; Women's Studies

Femininity, 94, 122–23, 140, 159. *See also* Feminist pedagogy: and femininity; Gender

Feminist Accused of Sexual Harrassment, 19, 20, 21, 67, 163

Foreclosure, 97, 157–58. *See also* Lacan, Jacques

Freud, Sigmund, 10–11, 100, 103, 167 n.3; on the interpretation of dreams, 10–11, 96; on sexuality, 10, 108–9. *See also* Psychoanalysis

Gay men, 41, 60

Gender: as performance, 110, 161, 171 n.3; vs. other sexual differences, 119–20, 125–26. *See also* Anecdote(s): and gender; Authority: and gender; Castration: and gender; Email: and gender; Femininity; Language: and gender; Masculinity; Pedagogy: and gender; Sexual harassment: and gender; Subjectivity: as gendered; Writing: and gender

Gender Studies, 26–27. *See also* Women's Studies

Generation(s), 4, 63, 112–14, 163

Genre. *See* Literature: and genre; Narrative

Getting Personal. See Miller, Nancy K.

Harlow, Barbara, 113, 117, 118, 169 n.1, 170 n.7

Hegel, G. W. F., 168 n.1

Heterosexism, 25. *See also* Homophobia; Sexual harassment: and heterosexism

Heterosexuality, 94, 159; as compulsory institution, 62. *See also* Heterosexism; Sexual harassment: and heterosexuality

Historicism, 89–91, 125, 169 n.2, 171 n.2

Historiography, 88, 157, 168 n.1

History: and anxiety, 90; and feminism, 35, 57, 64, 124–25, 139; of ideas, 58; of language, 125; and psychoanalysis, 11, 35; of teacher-student sex, 63; teleological nature of, 88–89, 168 n.1. *See also* Anecdote(s): and history; Narrative: and history; Writing: and history

Homophobia, 25. *See also* Heterosexism; Closet, metaphor of; Sexual harassment: and homphobia

Homosexuality. *See* Closet, metaphor of; Gay men; Homophobia; Lesbians; Sexual orientation; Sexual preference

Identity: and pedagogy, 30, 73, 80, 111; and sexual harassment, 18, 41; and women, 115–16, 125, 140

Identification, 94, 98, 141

Ideology. *See* Writing: and ideology

Imaginary, the, 35, 97. *See also* Lacan, Jacques

Jardine, Alice, 116–17

Johnson, Barbara, 95–98

Keyssar, Helene, 6, 26–35

Knowledge: and anxiety, 98; as intersubjective, 20–21, 163; and teaching, 65, 71, 110–11, 125; women's, 18, 52, 55–56, 63. *See also* Experience: and feminist epistemology; Pedagogy

Lacan, Jacques: on castration, 132; on foreclosure, 97; and Jacques Derrida, 10–11, 83–84, 93–99; on Oedipus, 100. *See also* Psychoanalysis

Language: and event, 2, 157; and gender, 122–23; history of, 124–25; and literary theory, 2, 10; and psychoanalysis, 8, 10, 133; and teaching, 105; and "theory," 1–2, 8, 11; and women, 113–26. *See also* Rhetoric; Translation; Writing

Law, 9, 55–57. *See also* MacKinnon, Catharine; Sexual harassment: and the law

Lecherous Professor, The, 16–18, 36–50

Lechery. *See* Sexual harassment: and lechery

Lesbians: and separatism, 151; and sexuality, 159; and teaching, 25, 29, 60, 68–71, 79

Literary theory, 1–2, 10, 22, 89, 91, 169 n.2

Literature, 1–2, 137; and genre, 3, 5. *See also* Narrative

Love. *See* Pedagogy: and love; Romance

MacKinnon, Catharine, 9, 45, 55–58, 61–62

Marriage, 27, 62, 69, 121, 124, 140

Masculinity, 94, 107, 133. *See also* Gender; Women: male-identified

Mastery: and anxiety, 98; as goal of "theory," 15–17, 22; and history, 126

McDaniel, Judith, 29, 31–32

Memoir, 14, 19

Memory, 99, 106, 169 n.1

Method, 16, 37, 39, 54, 79, 161; deconstructive, 7; feminist, 5, 6, 9, 23, 54–55; psychoanalytic, 10; scientific, 39, 42

Misogyny, 60

Miller, Nancy K., 156–64, 171 n.2

Miller, Susan, 27, 29, 33, 34

Modern Language Association (MLA), 77, 83, 90–91, 95, 127–34, 162–63

Morality: and eating, 147; and pedagogy, 104, 110–11; and pornography, 61; and sexual harassment, 41, 49–50, 57, 66; and teacher-student relations, 70–71; and women, 121. *See also* Ethics

Morgan, Robin, 139

Narrative: conventions of, 85, 104–5, 107, 110–11; and history, 82, 89; and teleology, 85–86, 88–89, 91–92, 157; and "theory," 1–2, 11, 16, 111. *See also* Anecdote(s): and narrative; History; Literature

New Historicism. *See* Historicism

Nietzsche, Friedrich. *See* Derrida, Jacques: on Friedrich Nietzsche

Object relations theory. *See* Chodorow, Nancy J.

Oedipus complex, 10; as triangular relation, 96–97. *See also* Freud, Sigmund; Lacan, Jacques

Origin: of *Anecdotal Theory,* 84; primal scene as, 106, 110

Passivity, 128–30

Pedagogy: and anecdotal theory, 4, 6–8, 19, 21, 35, 161; and conflict of interest, 67–80; and desire, 63, 65, 72, 75, 87–88, 103–9; eroticism of, 19, 21, 25–26, 29–30, 32, 53–54, 65, 69–70, 103, 106–8, 110; and gender, 24–27, 31–35, 107, 108, 109, 110; infantile, 108–10; and love, 29, 68–69, 71–76, 78, 103–6, 111; as performance, 87, 109–10; and romance, 69–74, 78–80, 105–6, 110. *See also* Anecdote(s): and pedagogy; Authority: and teaching; Ethics: in teaching; Feminist pedagogy; Identity: and pedagogy; Knowledge: and teaching; Language: and teaching; Romance; Sexual harassment: and education; Writing: teaching of

Penis. *See* Phallus

Personal, the, 18–21, 163–64. *See also* Anecdote(s): and the personal; Feminist pedagogy: and the personal; Miller, Nancy K.

Perversion, 10, 40, 58, 104

Phallocentrism, 93–94, 150. *See also* Lacan, Jacques

Phallus, 94, 151; as opposed to penis, 34. *See also* Lacan, Jacques

Pornography, 60–61

Positivism. *See* Empiricism

Pre-Oedipal, the, 35, 97. *See also* Imaginary, the; Lacan, Jacques

Primal scene, the. *See* Origin

Prostitution, 62, 116, 121

Protectionism, 57–58, 62–63

Psychoanalysis: and the academic job market, 129–34; and feminism, 10, 132–33. *See also* Anecdote(s): and psychoanalysis; Castration; Chodorow, Nancy J.; Deconstruction: and psychoanalysis; Foreclosure; Freud, Sigmund; History: and psychoanalysis; Imaginary, the; Lacan, Jacques; Language: and psychoanalysis; Oedipus complex; Perversion; Phallocentrism; Phallus; Pre-Oedipal, the; Repression; Subjectivity: psychoanalysis and; Symbolic, the; Uncanny, the

Psychology, 38, 42–43, 99, 129, 147

Race, 3, 125

Racism, 49

Reading: and connecting across difference, 136, 145, 150–52, 163–64; critical, 16, 22; Derrida on, 117–18; and pleasure, 105; and temporality, 135–36. *See also* Writing

Repression, 98–99, 166 n.8, 167 n.3. *See also* Freud, Sigmund

Rhetoric: and deconstruction, 5, 7; of email, 142, 149; and feminism, 4, 136–43, 149–52, 158–59; of homophobia, 41; and thought, 5, 138, 156–157. *See also* Language; Sisterhood; Writing

Rich, Adrienne, 26, 59, 62, 65

Rivalry: and feminism, 141, 153; sexual, 151; sibling, 139–40

Romance: conventions of, 105; as

between, 4, 119–20, 124–26, 143, 151, 161, 171 n.11; and education, 18, 23–35, 51–66; male-identified, 94, 169 n.1; Nietzsche on, 3, 112–26; as opposed to woman, 112–15, 119, 124–26. *See also* Experience: women's; Feminism; Feminist pedagogy; Identity: and women; Morality: and women; Protectionism; Sexuality: and women

Women's Studies, 26–27, 51–52, 55; men and, 27, 33. *See also* Feminism; Feminist pedagogy; Gender Studies

Writing: and audience, 82, 111, 135–38, 152; and connecting across difference, 136, 145, 150–52, 163–64; experimental, 2, 19, 160; and gender, 159–61; and history, 82, 88–89, 126; and ideology, 40, 167 n.3; occasional, 135–38; and style, 7, 40, 94, 105, 142–43; teaching of, 77–80, 101–3; as technology, 142, 145; and temporality, 22, 85–91, 105, 135–38, 157. *See also* Anecdote(s): and occasional writing; Dissemination; Language; Reading; Rhetoric

Jane Gallop is Distinguished Professor of English
and Comparative Literature at the University of
Wisconsin, Milwaukee. She is the author of several
previous books, including *Feminist Accused of
Sexual Harassment* (Duke University Press, 1997),
Around 1981: Academic Feminist Literary Theory
(1992), and *Thinking Through the Body* (1988).

Library of Congress Cataloging-in-Publication Data
Gallop, Jane.
Anecdotal theory / Jane Gallop.
p. cm.   Includes index.
ISBN 0-8223-3001-6 (cloth : alk. paper)
ISBN 0-8223-3038-5 (pbk. : alk. paper)
1. Feminist literary criticism. 2. Criticism. 3. Sexual harass-
ment in universities and colleges—United States. I. Title.
PN98.W64 G33 2002   801′.95′09048—dc21 2002003918